If you enjoy reading about Norfolk and Suffolk, Cambridgeshire and Essex, look for titles from 'Poppyland Publishing'.

Available at the time of printing:

The 'Albums' series

A Mundesley Album
A Cromer Album
A Sheringham Album
Sheringham - A Century of Change

The 'Norfolk Origins' series

Hunters to First Farmers
Roads and Tracks

Local history booklets

Great Yarmouth - History, Herrings and Holidays
Fakenham - Town on the Wensum
Holt - Historical Market Town
Coltishall - Heyday of a Broadland Village
Caister - 2000 Years a Village
The Cromer Lifeboats
Weybourne - Peaceful Mirror of a Turbulent Past
Have You Heard about Blakeney?
Salthouse - Village of Character and History
Cley - Living with Memories of Greatness
Poppyland - Strands of Norfolk History
The Hunstanton Lifeboats
Palling - A History Shaped by the Sea
Caister - Beach Boats and Beachmen

Many more titles are in preparation. For a current list, ask at your bookshop or write to Poppyland Publishing, 13, Kings Arms Street, North Walsham, Norfolk NR28 9JX

Those Seaside Days

MEMORIES OF EAST ANGLIAN FAMILY HOLIDAYS IN THE 1940's

Jean Grose

The 'East Anglian Memories' Series

© Jean Grose and Poppyland Publishing 1986

First Published 1986

ISBN: 0 946148 22 8

Designed, printed and bound by Speedprint, Spalding, Lincolnshire

Cover Design and illustration by Deeprose Design, Spalding, Lincolnshire

Contents

Introduction

When Jean Grose decided to write down the many memories of her childhood holidays, the intention was to pass on to her family the stories she had heard from her parents and grandparents; her recollections of those grandparents and the many happy holidays they spent together.

What resulted was not simply a recording of the events in the life of one family, but a story which captures the flavour of many family holidays in the 1940's. Though specific characters and places are mentioned, all who wish to recall holidays from that time will find their own experiences echoed here. And for readers who do not themselves recall that era, here is a valuable and enjoyable narrative, giving insight into the type of East Anglian holiday enjoyed by many in a time gone by.

To the visitor who has never travelled to an East Anglian resort other than by car, we begin our journey at Liverpool Street Station, with the hiss of steam and a through train to the coast. From the outset the story shows how much our lives have changed in the 40 years since the events recalled. We no longer have to make a jar of jam last a month, or pass through the gaps in the barbed wire to reach the beach!

However, throughout these memories the reader will find people and places, feelings and occasions that continue to be familiar and that are still to be found in seaside East Anglia. We are sure that in another 40 years time, there will be similar stories to recall the pleasures of such seaside days from those who are enjoying their youth now.

Main Line Train...

Liverpool Street Station! Dirty, smelly, smokey, noisy; the high Victorian building, heavy steel girders supporting a glass roof, the sunlight now obliterated by the years of steam and coal dust belched upwards by thousands of steam engines; but to the two little girls standing in the midst of the milling throng, sheer magic. Not for its own sake, although the hustle and bustle create an atmosphere of excitement which catches up everyone and scurries them along. This is a special place and today a very special day, the gateway to 'fairy-land' and the start of an annual journey, a pilgrimage.

They stand with their mother, dressed in their best blue costumes, white socks, black shoes and summer straw hats; their hair dressed in two long plaits hanging down their backs, tied with coloured ribbons at the ends. The younger one bobs up and down, chatting nineteen to the dozen. The other, quieter, more serious, tries to be grown-up and sensible, but the excitement and emotion within so intense, it's almost unbearable. She seems to boil up inside as she hugs her feelings to herself.

Platform nine, the long train of coaches stretching into the distance. Plenty of time yet to buy magazines and crossword books. Pencils and sweets are already tucked into school bags to help while away the hours.

On other platforms engines raise steam, the acrid smell bringing back all the happy memories of last year and the year before, and before!! Suddenly a spout of steam shoots upwards, accompanied by an earsplitting shriek. Everyone jumps and looks around for the offender. Having gained complete attention the monster quietens down to a steady chortle, awaiting the shrill whistle from the guard, giving permission to be on her way.

Empty lines, buffers red and shining, marking the end of the track, await trains from city and coast. Long trains with pink lamp-light windows, snaking around the last bend from the east end, proudly bringing their burden of holiday makers and business people from the ports of Harwich and The Hook. They glide into their allotted niches where porters wait with trolleys, and on reaching the buffers come to rest with contented sighs. The drivers, wiping their hands on greasy rags, their faces black and sweaty, sometimes a smile creasing the grime, climb down from the footplate. Steam twirls in wisps from the wheels of the monster engines, as though they too are happy to stand and cool off. Their long boiler bodies are shining black and dark green; their brass bright from loving care. Each tender, although piled high with black, dusty coal, is nevertheless polished and gleaming.

The girls and their mother are now choosing a carriage to be their home for the next three and a half hours. This must be done with care and earnest thought. The first priority is a table, if possible. These days, after the war, the dining cars are little used for their original purpose and passengers can sit at the tables for the complete journey. The seats, though faded and worn are still very plush and seem very large and enveloping to small figures. Sometimes there is a restaurant or buffet car on the train, and there is then the added excitement of one of their mother's old friends coming to talk to them. He will be in his tall white hat, maybe even bringing lunch or tea, making them very important persons. On one memorable occasion, early in the war, when the platform had been seething with uniforms and the corridors full with kit-bags, a chef had come to the door calling out their names and they had been escorted to seats reserved for them by a colleague of an uncle, also a railway chef.

Before deciding on a seat comes the problem of which end of the train is 'right'. Towards the end of the journey the last carriages will be slipped from their couplings to continue their travels on another branch line. So the choice of 'ends' is of paramount importance, the terrible fear of being left behind clouding their thoughts. The decision is made doubly difficult by the fact that the whole train runs into Norwich station, where a local engine is attached to the rear and then continues on its way in the reverse direction to a branch line, leaving the long distance engine at the buffers. A porter is usually consulted, just to be on the safe side!

At last they are settled; hats are taken off and the large suitcase, battered and strapped, stowed away. Books and pencil cases are dragged out, must not do too much at first, there is a long way to go.

This day has been anticipated for so long, worked for, counted to, the washing and ironing completed, shoes cleaned, buttons sewed on, bathing suits found and eventually everything packed away for a whole month, before having to return to a normal, everyday life, and back to school.

Their father has to stay and work for three more weeks and now that they are a little older their mother will be returning home to him, to join them in two weeks time. There is only one weeks holiday a year from the factory for him, and only with pay in the later years. So there is the added excitement of travelling alone, all be it they will have a good eye kept on them from the kitchen.

The hands of the station clock creep round towards 9.30 a.m. 'Goodbyes' and 'Take care!' are said and the bump and rattle as the engine is coupled to the front decides the girls' mother to stand out on the platform. Suddenly the guard's whistle pierces the air, doors slam, the green flag waves to the driver and with an answering 'toot-toot' and a jet of steam the engine takes up the strain, and slowly and sedately the long journey starts. The girls wave from the open window until their mother can no longer be seen on the platform and the train rounds the first bend, very steadily gathering speed as it crosses the many points and junctions, to settle onto the long distance track.

They close the window and with a happy sigh settle back in their seats. At last they are really on their way and soon they will be, once more, beside the sea.

...to Fairyland

It is now many years since those sunny, summer mornings. I suppose everyone was a little different, but there was continuity and the many memories roll together, making it difficult to assess whether a certain event happened each year, or just the once. We took this annual holiday for granted, assuming everyone had holidays, and even felt a little ashamed of always going to the same place, when other children spoke of different resorts. Not that we would have gone anywhere different had we been paid. I now realise how lucky we were, for so many families during and after the war were not able to have a holiday at all, and we spent a complete month with our maternal grandmother, without question.

Dad did not find it easy, and we certainly could not have afforded any other sort of holiday, but what more could children want. Nan was the most happy, caring person you could wish for. We knew how far we could try her, and a smacked bottom or clump with the hair brush was the reward for going too far. 'Don't be brunny!' she would chide us if we became too excitable. At the same time we had freedom! Our comings and goings fell into a regular pattern around meal times; we always knew where to go when we were hungry, but we were not expected to have adult supervision all the time.

'Off to the beach with you, whilst we make the beds, and we'll come and find you,' was the morning cry. 'I can get on better once you are all out of the way,' was my grandmother's favourite expression.

'All' were cousins, aunts and uncles and usually a couple of dogs. I don't suppose, in fact I know, we were not all there every year, but the memories are of a house full of 'family'. I think everyone tried to go 'home' sometime during August and there were many occasions when we overlapped. How we all fitted in I do not know, but from the children's point of view, it was great fun; and, judging by the laughter and banter around us, none of the 'grown-ups' were complaining either.

The train chugged on its way, through Stratford, Ilford and Romford once more. We had already travelled this route to London and now had to retrace our steps as the 'Norfolkman' did not stop until Colchester, or possibly Ipswich. We discussed who might be coming down and when, whether to do some colouring or read a book. There was always an 'Enid Blyton' to enjoy. My sister's favourite, though, was the 'Main-Line Train to Fairyland', and that I suppose was how we felt about this journey. The contrast between departure and arrival was, to us, like being transported to another world.

We left London, slowly passing dirty little houses, many still showing bomb damage, blackened net curtains flapping at glassless window frames, grey slate roofs; factories, steel yards, tiny gardens with bare-patched squares of grass, children hot and tired watching the train go by. Once Romford had been passed we felt we were getting somewhere. The wheels were chattering now and settling into the steady 'diddle-e-dee diddle-e-dum' rhythm over the track joints. Telegraph wires rose and fell as post after post flashed by the window. Now and then the engine called out as she passed a station or signal box. 'Whoo-Whoo. Here we come! Here we come!' Smuts flicked in at the slightly open window and the smell of burning soot reached our nostrils.

Soon we were in the open countryside. I know now it was only Shenfield, not so very far from where we lived, but this was the only time we came this way, so it was the beginning of the journey proper to us.

The fields were golden with corn, ripening fast under the August sun. Harvesters were at work in some of the fields, though not the great combines of today. There were more people around, pitching and baling. Cows and horses glanced up as we thundered past, most unconcerned at the monster running along the edge of their field. Sometimes a young one would kick up its heels and shy away to the opposite corner. People stood at level-crossing gates, chatting to the crossing-keeper whilst waiting to continue along the lane once we had passed by. On occasions they smiled and waved to the little girl standing at the window, dreaming as the fresh air rushed by her face, the breath taken from her if she leaned a fraction further out. Her hair streamed back, and she was filled with the joy of anticipation, singing quietly to herself as she savoured this journey, the prelude to all she had dreamed of during the last eleven months.

I stand sometimes now at a level crossing-gate, waiting for a train to pass, so that I may continue my walk along the lane. It may be one which I used to look down upon from my window, but the trains are now pulled by throbbing diesels, without the character or back-chat of our steam engines.

'Here I come, clear the way, mustn't be late' they seemed to say, smoke streaming from the funnel, enjoying the thrill of the race along the track as much as the passengers ... at least, those who bothered to listen.

The beautiful summer countryside rolled past, huge trees breaking up the lines of green hedges around the golden fields. Oaks, elms, poplars, chestnuts, I did not know their names, but loved the wide spreading branches making shady oases for the animals. Sometimes a rabbit would scurry for its burrow; and everywhere crows and rooks chattered and squabbled. But then, so did we two sisters when we had a mind, though today all is sweetness and light.

The Norfolk border has now been crossed. London, Essex and Suffolk are behind us and the wide blue East Anglian sky, stretching to the horizon, is dotted with white, wispy clouds, their outlines ever changing from little dogs, horses heads, witches faces, to giants, dragons and castles. The countryside is spread wide as far as the eye can see, farm houses and barns clustered here and there among the rich golden corn. A tall Norfolk church tower points skywards, its solid flint walls a landmark to be seen for miles, a monument to richer days, when Norfolk had a thriving woollen industry. Many villages which grew up in the shadow of the flint towers have now dwindled to no more than hamlets, the churches left to dream of their former glories, the winds whistling around their pinnacles, but making little impression, even after hundreds of years blowing across from the North Sea. Sometimes five, six or seven churches can be spotted at one time.

The rhythm of the wheels changes, there is a gentle slowing down of the train, and we realise we are approaching Norwich station. The city comes as a surprise after the many miles of open country. A factory, still wearing its war-time camouflage paint of brown and khaki, stands along the side of the track, which now opens up into a network of lines, interlacing one with another to enter sidings, goods yards and onto other branch lines. The train picks its way over the points and slides into Thorpe Station.

There were times when up to an hour had to pass before we could be on our way again, and then great aunts and cousins would come and sit with us. Their homes were on the outskirts of the city and it was pleasant to chat over a cup of tea; invitations were issued to 'come to lunch next week' and their strong Norfolk brogue made us feel we were in another world, after what we considered to be the 'plain' accents of our Essex neighbours.

Today, however, there is only a ten minute break and then we feel the bump of the local engine going on at the rear and we are pulled out, seemingly the way we have just come, but we notice the London line bearing off to our right and we take the bend and head for the coast.

The rhythm changes suddenly to a rumble as we cross a bridge, one of many, over a part of the Broads. The water reflects the blue of the sky and cabin cruisers are moored along the banks, the sun sparkling on their varnished decks and brass rails. The white sail of a yacht appears to be riding the waves of a corn field. The reeds at the water's edge meet the barley along these narrow waterways. A few windmills are dotted about, most no more than ruined shells.

Sleepy little stations drowse as we pass. The London train is of no interest to them, for only the locals stop at their platforms. They might be in need of a coat of paint and a bit of attention to the rust on the cast iron work holding up the canopies, but the war put a stop to such extravagance. However, their gardens are ablaze with colour, loving care giving a glow of welcome to all who come and go. There are flower-beds edged with flint stones, often painted white, to frame the multi-coloured picture within. Many have their names picked out with flowers or white washed stones.

Now is the time for us to start packing up our books and pencils. An excursion along the corridor to the toilet, not so many people left in the compartments now, the engine singing along its familiar lines. Our hands washed, hair tidied, ribbons re-tied, jackets on again, and, with the case standing by the door, we are ready, excited grins spreading on our faces.

We stop at North Walsham station and then on to Gunton. At this point, after leaving the station, we slow to a crawl and the rear section of the train is slipped off at the junction, to be picked up and taken on around the coast.

The few coaches now left gather speed again, but we are almost there. We round the last bend, two heads craning out of the window to compete for the first sight of the lighthouse, standing white and bright out on the cliff-top. Having the extra height, I can usually claim this privilege, unless my attention wavers. 'There it is!' we cry with pleasure and, almost immediately, 'There's the water-tower!' This old cast iron tower on the hill just outside the town, and then past the signal box and we are running into the platform. 'I wonder who will be there to meet us?' We hang out of the window searching for a familiar face. Sometimes we are met, sometimes not; it does not matter, we know the way to go.

Tumble out onto the platform with our bits and pieces, no hurry, this is the end of the line. The air is sharp and fresh after the stuffy carriage and even stuffier London. Clump across the bare boards of the old ticket office, into the forecourt of the station. It is not called 'The High' for nothing. Built on top of the hill which climbs steadily out of the town it commands a splendid view and extends a wonderful welcome. The blue sky forms a canopy, dropping down to merge with the blue-green sea, a panorama with white horses prancing in the distance. In the foreground the town nestles in its hollow, with the great square tower of the church standing out and above everything. 'There's the church!' we shout with satisfaction. All is as it should be. We are back in Cromer!

Number 9

Our grandparents home was one of many terraced houses, built around the turn of the century, on Suffield Park. Just outside the town of Cromer, this had obviously formed part of the estate of Lord Suffield. When our mother was a child the whole area had many large houses and estates owned by extremely well-to-do people. They too used to come from London for the summer and, although their background and circumstances were so different from our own, their pleasure could not have exceeded ours as we stood on the long slope leading from Cromer High Station down to the Suffield Hotel, from where we could survey the whole of Suffield Park. Streets of little red-brick houses were tucked together under the grey slate roofs, which after a shower of rain gleamed steel blue under the sun. We would try to pick out our grandmother's from the rest but it took time, and we were anxious now to be down there and see her smiling face.

Grasping the thick leather handle of the old suitcase, which usually had a couple of tennis racquets strapped to the outside, I heaved it up against my thigh, and we set off. My sister struggled with our satchels and handbags. Grandad sometimes met us with his green wooden 'wheelbarrow', a box on wheels with two long handles, which he had 'knocked up' and which served many useful purposes.

Down the slope, avoiding the three-wheeled L.N.E.R. parcels van, which spluttered up and down the hill. The station was very convenient for people living in or visiting 'the Park', but was a good distance from the town and hotels. Cromer Beach Station, set on the other side of town, was better placed, bringing people streaming in from the Midlands, but we felt it a very inferior station to ours; our track went all the way to London, and their view was not nearly so breath-taking.

Put the case down, have a breather, change hands, on past the fish and chip shop. Oh! the thought of those hot, vinegared chips, salt sticking to the fingers; must have a bag tonight before bed-time. I don't think we tasted chips for the rest of the year. There was the 'Goat Field', no goats now, but the old name had stuck. We played football and cricket there and squeaked for hours on the two old swings hanging from their rusty frames. 'Vincent's', the corner shop, brought us in view of 'Number 9' and at last we were going up the passageway to the back gate. No-one used the front door, except the parson and the undertaker.

The terrace of houses was divided at intervals by a passage leading to the back gardens of ten or so houses. This passage formed a tunnel beneath the upper storey of one house and our grandmother lived in the house to the right. It was a grand place for bouncing balls and had a marvellous echo. The habit had been formed over the years to announce our arrival by calling out 'Dish it up' or 'Pour it out', our voices reverberating around us as we scuffed the loose stones in the soft earth. What the very ladylike neighbour, whose home formed the other half and roof of the tunnel, thought of this, I shudder to remember, but as children we thought it great fun and as our father was the biggest culprit, no-one could chide us for our bad manners.

Lift up the latch on the high wooden gate and Nan's voice would reach us as she spied us through the scullery window. 'Here they are then! Come on in my beauties. Drop that old case down there.' A big hug and a kiss and, suddenly feeling a little shy, into the old familiar room, well worn and smelling of polish; the range blacked, brass knobs shining and the aroma of rabbit pie wafting from the oven by the fire. Flop down onto the old blue leather sofa behind the table. Remembering to pass on the messages and love our mother had sent with us, we gazed around the room to spot any changes. The walls were covered with photographs; all the family weddings, a large framed group of our grandparents with their five children, and in the alcove by the door leading to the front of the house, another large portrait of four generations of females. My grandmother, with her first-born in long white gown on her lap, flanked by her mother and grandmother. All the ladies in tight waisted, high busted gowns, with leg-o'-mutton sleeves and the most enormous flowered hats. All of them looking very serious, proud and formidable.

Grandad's certificate of Honourable Discharge from the Army, the First World War, hung behind us, and the shelves across the other alcove of the fire-place were cluttered with smaller snapshots, in their individual frames, of all the newer members of the family. The babies on their rugs, the toddlers with their toys. We were there somewhere! A large radio competed with a few books for the remaining space. I remember the accumulator of the radio had to be taken periodically to the local ironmonger to be recharged, and very heavy it was too.

On the high mantleshelf over the range, with its ever burning fire and black kettle simmering on the hob, stood tea caddy, letters, rent and insurance books, and at either end the black and white china spaniels which graced all the family homes of the period. Another door, to our left, led into the large pantry cupboard under the stairs.

The scullery we had walked through from the back yard had a shallow, brown stone sink with one cold water tap, the only tap in the house. A kitchen towel on a wooden roller hung behind the back door. In the corner was a brick built boiler, under which a fire could be lit for wash day, although I do not remember this being in use by the time we came on the scene; there was also a small fireplace and alongside this a gas stove. This my grandmother used on occasions, especially when there was a house full, but she scorned it for its inefficiency compared with the oven in her old range. 'That don't make my 'Yorkshires' rise as they ought,' she would grumble.

By now she would be 'dishing up.' My grandmother's rabbit pie was out of this world. Her pastry was pale and crisp and I have never found anyone who could make it in the same way. Grandad used to breed his own rabbits in hutches on his allotment. They were kept warm and dry and well fed. 'He care more about his old rabbits than he do for me,' grandmother would laugh. We loved to feel their soft fur and watch them wrinkle their noses at the carrots we offered. Now I shudder at the thought but, as children, we did not seem to connect the rabbit pie with the lovely creatures in their hutches, although we knew grandad 'grew' them and we were very grateful when he sent one home for us, especially during the war-time meat rationing. He would tie a label on its leg and post it to our mother, who would skin and then bake it with onion rings and potatoes. No chicken was whiter or more full of flavour than those 'home-grown' rabbits. I have never enjoyed one since. We even had little fur collars made from the pelts which kept us warm in winter.

We 'gathered round the festive board,' always a crisp white table-cloth. The cutlery and china may have been old and well worn, but everything was spotless. My grandmother never lowered the standards with which she had been brought up, even when money was tight, and she detested thick china and glass.

Having loaded our plates, she sat herself at the corner of the table. I can never remember her having her own meal with us. I suppose she ate quietly on her own when our needs had been satisfied. She bobbed up and down from range to table, out to the scullery and then sat with us whilst we 'licked our platters clean.' My clearest picture of her is seated at the corner of the table, her hands around the old brown teapot on its metal stand, her rings tapping against its side. I think her wedding ring had either worn too thin or perhaps had been used during a spell of hardship, but I only remember her wearing what must have been a dress ring, without its stone, twisted round to look like a plain band. On their golden wedding day grandad gave her a new wedding ring amidst much laughter about making an honest woman of her at last. I wish I knew the story behind the wearing of the ring without its jewel.

Pudding was always served in blue and white dishes with a rim around the edge, which was perfect for plum stones, and we always played Tinker, Tailor, Soldier, Sailor, losing or borrowing unashamedly to make it come out 'right' according to our fancy at the time.

Sometimes we would have a plain suet pudding with warm golden syrup, as light as a feather. We were always amused to see that grandad had his 'pudding' first with gravy and followed this with a course of meat and vegetables. As children we could not understand this, but now realise that in his younger days meals were served in this way to take the edge off the appetite and so enable the meat to go further. Grandad still retained this habit and it was the same with his Sunday roast, always the Yorkshire pudding with gravy first. He preferred plain meals, no fancy made-up dishes or even a shepherd's pie, which he scathingly referred to as 'messances'. He sat opposite our grandmother, in his kitchen chair with the high back and curved arms; a little man with a full moustache - which he insisted was all the better for a good oiling with kipper grease - a quiff of hair licked over his forehead, and a wicked twinkle in his eye. He would wrinkle his little button of a nose, in perfect imitation of his rabbits, making us laugh when we should have been eating, then we would all be told off for messing about at the table. Nevertheless, if grandad said 'No' you did not argue.

Through the door in the far corner was the staircase, straight up between the front and back rooms. The hand-rail was lovely for rolling small balls up and down, until grandmother chivvied us to 'stop playing about on those stairs, someone will get hurt.' Living in a bungalow eleven months of the year, we were fascinated by stairs and especially by the shell-shaped brass light switches top and bottom, controlling the one lamp. We thought this very clever.

The front room was not used a great deal, although it was not barred to us as in some homes we knew. The over-mantle was a joy to explore; there were many elaborately carved shelves all backed with small mirrors, and painted the usual 'Victorian' dark green, as was most of the woodwork in the house. Each square inch of space was taken up with the small pieces of white china painted with the coats of arms of the various towns or resorts they represented. 'A Present from ...' There were miniature watering cans, lighthouses, monuments, dogs, churches, cheese dishes.

Two large black and white prints dominated one wall, which I found very poignant and sentimental. 'Sorrow' depicted a mother and child, telegram in hand, faces sad and drawn; a newspaper lay on the table, the headlines telling of the losses suffered during a particular battle of the war. 'Joy' showed them throwing up their arms, faces radiant, as they welcomed a wounded, but very much alive young soldier, coming through the door. A lump came to my throat, even as a child, as I stood looking at them.

Upstairs were three bedrooms and a long landing. Nan and grandad normally used the middle room and we children usually squeezed into the little back room. The front room always seemed large, full of light and was considered the 'best room'. We used to joke about which members of the family were to be privileged to sleep there. All the beds were the brass-knobbed bedsteads which the last generation could not wait to throw out, and which today are much appreciated. They were all covered with snowy white, honeycombed, cotton bedspreads. Marble-topped washstands held white china jug, basin and soap dish sets, with a glass carafe and tumbler. Underneath stood the matching chamber pot and enamel slop pail.

Each room had a wardrobe and mahogany chest-of-drawers, again items we took for granted and which now we would dearly love to possess. On the bow-fronted chests, with their lace-edged runners, stood dressing glasses, swing mirrors on mahogany bases, some with a miniature drawer beneath.

Heavy white lace covered the sash windows, with roll-up blinds behind. We had many a ticking-off for jerking these up and down and making them flap against the windows; then of course they would stick in the roller and move neither up nor down!

Over the cast iron mantleshelf of the small fireplace in the front bedroom was a large coloured print of a painting of 'Ruth' gleaning in the fields. As we were mostly on holiday during the whole of the month of August, this particular picture seemed most appropriate, as everywhere we went the fields were golden with ripe corn or dusty with harvesting, stooks set out, row upon row, to dry before stacking.

Beneath the picture on the narrow shelf stood three porcelain ornaments. In the centre was a pure white statuette of a young girl in some form of peasant costume, the head-dress reminiscent of a Dutch hat with its side wings. She stood beside a small round cart with large wheels, drawn by a small horse or goat. My memory deserts me, although I can see the sweep of her arm along its back as she half turns to the side.

A matching pair stood either side of the goat girl, a young girl and a young man in the romantic clothes of the Regency period. As though poised in their respective cottage doorways, framed by creepers, they peeped at each other, the girl demure and coquettish, the lad bold in his cocked hat and breeches. The two pieces were actually vases, although I never saw them put to this use. The texture and colour were as icing sugar, the clothes picked out in palest pinks, blues and greens, with little cherub faces.

I adored those little people and would sometimes dare to trace my finger over them, but they seemed so delicate I was afraid to handle them. I must have made my grandmother aware of my love for them at some time, which was unusual; I normally kept my feelings to myself (my sister was the exuberant one) but I can remember her saying 'When I have gone, my beauty, they are yours.'

Having revisited the whole house, sorted out 'our room' and dragged a few things from the case, we would change from our smart little travelling costumes, stand our best shoes under the wash stand and throw on something light and comfortable. On our feet our school P.T. plimsoles, which we would live in until they disintegrated around our toes.

All ready now, a quick goodbye to Nan, and 'see you teatime,' and we were away, her voice following us down the passage 'Do you mind how you go now my loves!'

Familiar Places Revisited

Now we were heading for our first really good look at the sea. Along the road, round the corner, up the hill and into the woods. A flight of shallow steps; one, two, three, one, two, three, as we tried to run up them, keeping the rhythm, but the slope was too long and our legs tired. On our left the Warren Woods, thick and green, hiding the many paths we loved to scamper along; in the centre an old well, which I was told used to generate power for the hotel, many years before. The old, broken cover enabled us to drop stones down and count the seconds before the faint splash was heard, making us shudder at the thought of the long, dark, dank passage!

The woods smelt of wild garlic, not everyone's choice, but so dear to our memories that no rose smelt sweeter or conjured up happier thoughts. I had never noticed the smell anywhere else until, a few years ago, we climbed the wooded hillside to the Castle of Lichenstein, and I was immediately transported and reminded that familiar and loved places are equally as exciting as those which are new with the exotic sounding names.

High on the hill to our right, with views over the Royal Cromer Golf Links, stood the old Royal Links Hotel. Behind its high brick wall, the drive climbing in terraced sweeps, it stood a symbol of past grandeur and elegance, before war changed the way of life for so many. We only knew it as a massive barracks for the many soldiers we saw passing to and fro, and who on departure left training ropes and nets hanging from many of the trees, a wonderful, ready made playground for agile children. We waved to the soldiers as they stood in the sunshine at open windows, polishing their huge black boots and whitening their belts and gaiters. We watched sometimes as they dragged massive guns on carriages up and down the lighthouse slopes, where the turf, even today, is pitted and spoilt, and we found it all terribly exciting.

After the war the hotel was refurbished and an effort made to restore its glory but an electrical fire one night gutted and destroyed it. The site was cleared and has since been used for holiday caravans and now chalets. I am sure few holidaymakers know its history and certainly even fewer could afford to stay in the place as it was. We must be happy so many continue to enjoy the magnificent views and children can still scamper down the hill to the beach by way of valley and cliffs, through gorse bushes and the sweet nutty scent of the broom, all of which were once restricted to the lucky few.

All that remains visible today is the brick wall surrounding the terraced drive. Commencing at about 18 inches high it rises gently to around 12 or 15 feet. As Grandad would have said, 'That go up a fair depth.' A handrail surmounts it, leaving a sloping edge of about six inches on either side.

Naturally this presented a challenge to us all. Very seldom did we walk the lower path; always as we reached the top of the steps we automatically clambered onto the wall, bathing bundles under our arms, and edged our way to the far end. I suppose it was about the length of a football pitch. We progressed as our legs and daring grew from walking on the inside where the path followed the incline to almost scampering along on the outside, barely using the handrail, high above our parents. We looked down on them with scorn and pity, on the boring old path. As we reached the far end the length of bricks and mortar seemed to inbed itself in an earth wall and the trees took over. We would find a path and race each other down to the rest of the family - if they were with us. I am sure my mother and her brothers and sisters when young walked the wall as we did, with all our cousins, and since that time our own children have found the same pleasure. Fortunately there was never a slip, but I have seen holidaymakers watching with their hearts in their mouths. Even our dogs took pride in joining us, nimble on their four feet and no hands with which to hold on. Once, I am told, our little black and white terrier pranced merrily along and on reaching the highest point suddenly realised that his master and mistress were way below him. So, to their horror, he jumped down to join them, landed neatly, shook himself and trotted off again. They could not believe he had not broken every bone in his body.

Passing Happy Valley, with the lighthouse presiding over all, we reached the edge of the cliff. We were breathless in our haste to see the sea and guessing whether the tide would be 'in' or 'out.' My memory is always of it 'out.' The sun sparkled off the tiny ripples lapping at the water's edge, and reflected on the ridged, damp sand stretching as far as the eye could see, from Overstrand to the east to Cromer pier and town to the west, broken only by the black line of a breakwater. The lighter, softer sand above high tide mark, bordered by a ribbon of flint stones, holding tiny pools left behind by the receding water. More grey and white stones, warm and dry in the sun and then the sandy cliffs rising magnificently to the sky. Little white clouds, looking like puff balls, floated overhead, the cliffs were green with rabbit-cropped grass; there were gorse and bramble bushes and the odd path of golden sand threaded its way down.

Little figures dotted the beach, so small and colourful with their rubber balls and kites, but their voices rising amazingly clearly as the breeze lifted the children's delighted shrieks and the dogs' happy yaps to those standing way above them. We drank in the beauty, with the happiness and anticipation of running down the sandy path to join the scene. The salty tang stung our nostrils as the breeze swept back our hair and lifted our skirts, urging our legs to take off and run and run.

These of course were the days after the war when the beach and cliffs were once more ours to enjoy. We had had our holidays in war-time; in fact we spent more time, perhaps, than before in Norfolk, which was considered a safer area than our own, only twenty miles from London. But our father had had to remain at his job in the factory and our mother could not settle to be away from him for too long. Not knowing what each day would bring, we would go home after a short rest, to be all together.

I can remember one occasion sitting on grandmother's sofa for what seemed to be half of the night, listening to the throbbing roar of aeroplane engines, heavy guns and occasionally the distant thudding of bombs dropping. As our mother said, it was worse than being at home as we seemed to be in the direct route to and from Germany that night. Indeed we were, for that was the night Coventry was devastated.

Cromer suffered its fair share of casualties, Woolworths and one or two other shops being damaged. Many windows in the parish church were completely destroyed by the blast and part of the 1914-1918 War Memorial with its statuettes was badly broken. During these years the cliff-tops and beaches were forbidden territory. Barbed wire coiled its way along our cliff walks, the beach was mined and the poor pier had a gaping hole blown in its centre as a deterrent in case of a German invasion. It looked so sad and neglected.

We were allowed to use one small section of the beach, near the town, and as much as possible life went on, and holidaymakers swam and played in the sun. We were too young to remember what times had been like before the war so we accepted the limited access and the longer walk to the beach. It was just another case of 'Don't forget there is a war on!' We did not clamour for non-existent ice creams, because we had forgotten what ice cream tasted like, although we must have enjoyed plenty of them before the war. Grandfather had been a 'Stop me and Buy One' salesman at one time. We have a photograph of myself perched on top of his tricycle, with the cold box in front, almost hidden beneath his white 'Wall's' cap with its shiny black peak. When times did begin to improve one of the tea shops in the town was attracting new customers by serving the first post-war ice creams. We had been in with the family and so enjoyed the creamy vanilla and sharp, fruity raspberry flavours, that my sister and I decided to be very grown up and treat ourselves to an afternoon ice-cream one day when we were out on our own. We gave our order and lingered over the delicious home-made confection in the fancy glass dishes. Then the waitress presented us with the bill. We were horrified to find that eating in fancy tea shops was far more expensive than a cornet from the corner shop, and after digging deep into our pockets had to confess we did not have enough money to pay for them. The waitress gave us a lecture about ordering food without checking we could afford it first, and we promised to bring the remainder after we had been home to get some more money. Although very stern she did, however, tell us we need not bother ourselves to do that, and we escaped; but we never did forget the humiliation and embarrassment of our first attempt to be 'grown-up'.

One of the first tasks in those days of the war and after, on arriving in Cromer, was to run down to the Food Office to 'change' our ration books. Everyone was registered with certain local tradesmen and issued with the appropriate coupons enabling them to buy basic commodities. As we stayed with our grandmother for three or four weeks it was necessary to re-register with her tradesmen. Until this was done she could not go shopping, whatever money she might have in her purse. Her own rations would not stretch for long to satisfy our healthy, young, appetites. We enjoyed being trusted to carry out this task; not only did it make us feel important, but it also made us feel less that we were casual visitors and more like residents.

Some years after the war one of the offices used by the Ministry of Food, was converted back again to the booking office for the putting greens. Although much older, as I chose my club for a game, in my minds eye I could see two little girls rushing in with their ration books, happy to tell the food officer they had come to stay with their Nan who was waiting to go shopping.

There were several shops scattered about on Suffield Park; two or three were general stores, which really did seem to sell everything. There was a post office and stationers which was always referred to as the 'Dairy'. It never occurred to us that it sold everything except dairy produce. It was always called the dairy so it was the 'Dairy'

Vincent's corner shop was situated only four doors away from 'Number 9' and Nan would pop on her hat, pick up her wicker basket, and, smoothing her overall, trot along each day to purchase whatever was necessary for our almost insatiable appetites. Most days it was as far as she would go, but there was always someone to chat with, a baby to admire, an elderly neighbour with whom to commiserate or a tradesman to chivvy or share a joke. Often a young grandson would come running up the passage with a message from his father, hopefully looking for a boiled sweet or a biscuit as a reward.

I always see her smiling and nodding to folks as she made her short 'progress' to the corner, her long hair, thinning now, neatly coiled on the nape of her neck, under her everyday hat of navy or plum coloured felt. The hat would be pierced with the most wicked-looking hat pins to keep it in place. These were about six inches long, perhaps with a large pearl-type knob. They were pinned to the hat when not in use, removed before wear, and whilst pushing one into place she would hold the other between her lips, like a miniature pirate's cutlass, often admonishing us at the same time to hurry up and get our shoes on.

I don't think she would have dreamed of going out of the gate without her hat on, winter or summer, and it was a standing joke that after an outing she never thought to remove it. The kettle would go on and the table be laid, even bread and butter cut with her hat still bobbing on her head. When teased about it she would say that whilst she had her hat on she was ready in case of callers. 'If it is someone I am happy to see, I can say 'Do come in - I have just got here myself.' Anyone I want to be rid of, 'I am so sorry - I was just on my way out!' Not being one to hurt anyones feelings I can well believe that she used this harmless trick on occasions. Her frocks and shoes were typical of the times for ladies of her generation; longish skirts and stout shoes, but she never dressed in what we thought of as 'old granny clothes'. She hated black and although materials were suitably sombre for her age, they were always sprigged with flowers or edged with a white collar, and never did she consider herself 'dressed' without a square of lace pinned into the top of her bodice, her 'modest' as she called it, held in place by a small metal brooch forming 'Mother'. One dress, kept for very special occasions over many years, was what she laughingly called her 'delphinium blue', quite a daring colour for an elderly lady at that time, but she had no time for 'old fogies'.

We were all well known at the corner shop. My mother, having grown up in the same road, was always welcomed with open arms. 'How are you my beauty? You're looking well. My how the children have grown. That little'un looks just as cheeky as you were at her age!' We were often sent along for the odd item suddenly needed and that shop smelt like no other I have been in ever since. The wooden floorboards and the long varnished counter, rows upon rows of shelves, glass cases, sacks on the floor, little stacks of wood for firing, vegetables, butter and cheese on their marble slabs and through the archway the butchers section; the spicy smell of sausages mingling with the scent of the sawdust on the floor - you could scuff all sorts of patterns in it as you waited to be served. Those sausages were out of this world. They were so full of meat, minced coarse enough to chew, not like the slime of so many of today's products. The herbs and spices combined to make your mouth water. They were so fat and full it was difficult to cook them without the skins bursting. Charlie, the young butcher, learning the trade at this time, was tall with thick black curly hair, and had a happy twinkle in his eye. He was a little diffident and shy, but always pleased to see us, and have a joke. So the sausages came to be called 'Charlie's Sausages.' No one could make them to equal his and over the next thirty-five years we would not dream of going to Cromer without purchasing a few pounds of Charlie's Sausages to bring back and share around the family. He moved to another shop in the town, although owned by the same family, and we followed him. But now Charlie has retired, and soon after the old firm closed their premises. We have not found another business using anything like his recipe, so we must be satisfied with the tantalising memory of the gorgeous aroma of Charlie's sausages frying over the fire, and the lovely story my mother tells of a Christmas before we were born. The family had gathered together, sausages had been bought, by the yard I should think, to satisfy all, but not one could be found when Nan went to the meat safe. Then she heard giggling from the dining room, and went in to find that an uncle, her son-in-law, had festooned the room by stringing up the sausages in loops along the picture rail. I can imagine her mobbing at them, calling them a lot of silly fools, whilst she was almost helpless with laughter herself.

She would purse her lips so tightly to simulate anger but behind her little round, steel rimmed spectacles her blue eyes would be dancing with delight. Her skin, as I remember, was a little wrinkled by now; of course, she was in her sixties and had had a fairly hard life, but it was very soft and mellow. In fact she was a little apple-dumpling person, small and round, not fat but cosy. On her chin was a little soft wart, which she called her 'wimple.' We loved it; she would not have been the same person without it and it seemed to accentuate her joy of life and sense of fun when she laughed.

Being a true Norfolk woman stew and dumplings were, of course, a speciality. Those dumplings were so light it was difficult to imagine they were made from flour and suet. I am told that in true Norfolk style she could make them without the aid of suet and still produce a light, fluffy dumpling, but neither I nor my mother have any idea how she did it. Sometimes she would send someone to the bakehouse for a piece of dough, and that made the most delicious dumplings when popped on top of a gently simmering rabbit stew. Accompanied by newly dug, home-grown potatoes, carrots, broad beans or peas, is it any wonder the food of today appears to have lost much of its flavour?

Backgrounds

My grandparents home was a quite ordinary terraced Edwardian house, well furnished, but well used. They had not had much money to spare over the years, five children to feed and clothe and two more had been fostered at one period. Grandad had worked hard at his boot and shoe business and all his spare time went on his allotment, caring for his rabbits and growing all his own vegetables. So, although cash might not have been readily to hand, they were all well fed with good fresh meat and greens.

During the 1914-18 War he was caught in a mustard gas attack in the trenches and, due to the damage to his lungs, he was discharged from the Army, after a long convalescence. He recovered to a great extent, but found the atmosphere of leather and polish aggravating to his lungs, and he had eventually to give up his little shop in Hans Place, between the cinema and the corner greengrocers. He spent the remainder of his working life doing odd jobs, building work, road work, ice-cream salesman and golf-caddy. Until he was well into his seventies, he used to go caddying at the golf club. He was such a little man, I do not know how he managed to 'lug' the clubs around. You could almost have popped him into one of the bags, but he liked the atmosphere and the exercise, and appeared to be very popular. He had quite a list of regular 'gentlemen' who would ask for his services.

He evidently came from a fairly poor home, his father having moved to Norwich from Scotland to find work. Hence the name 'Muirhead' in the heart of the Norfolk countryside. It was a family joke that my grandmother had married beneath her, but she certainly never regretted allowing the shabby lad in the heavy working boots to pay her court after having the nerve to follow a young lady home after church one Sunday. They thought the world of each other in their own quiet, casual way. 'If he should call me 'darling' I would think he had had one too many,' she would say. 'We don't need to make a lot of fuss and palaver. If he calls me a silly old 'B' I know he still loves me.'

I can quite understand how she was attracted to him, his was such an extrovert personality. He was always telling jokes and making up stories, we never knew what was the truth. He came home with such yarns about people he was supposed to have met and things he had seen. 'Go on with you, you old fool!' Nan would lovingly chide him, 'Filling up their heads with your old squit.' 'Ah,' he would chuckle, 'Half my lies aren't true!'

I think he would have loved to have been in show business. Whenever there was an amateur concert or people invited on stage from the audience during the local music hall shows, he was always the first one up there. He had a pleasant singing voice and would have made a marvellous little comedian. He loved 'Happy Drome' on the radio with the three comics Ramsbottom, Enoch and Me; his humour was as theirs.

Whenever he was introduced to anyone he would step forward, grasp their hand in his and say 'I am, aren't you?' There was just no answer to that and their polite 'How-do-you-do' was swallowed whilst they attempted to assess this dapper little man, with the beautiful button-hole, which he always wore, and the twinkle in his eye.

He was a stickler for keeping 'best' clothes and shoes smart and tidy. Boots were regularly inspected and mended and his good suit always carefully brushed and hung up again in the cupboard. When 'formally' dressed he always wore a waistcoat complete with pocket watch and chain, holding one or two silver coins, looped across his front; in his buttonhole a fragrant rose or sweet-pea embellished with a minute spray of fern, all kept fresh and lasting in its own holder. This was a metal tube which clipped onto the buttonhole and hung behind his lapel, allowing the stems to be in water all the time. Winter and summer, he was never without a flower or spray of some sort. When not in use the holder had its own little stand on the sideboard where the flower could remain upright, like a miniature vase.

Whenever there was time for a rest he would sit in his old 'grandfather's' chair, spectacles perched on the end of his nose, a 'Woodbine' stuck between his lips and enjoy a good book. Ash would drop on his trousers as he puffed away at his cigarette and many an old pair had tiny little scorch marks where the ends dropped off when he became engrossed in the story. The centre of his moustache was yellowed with nicotine and I am sure scorched by his frugal habit of smoking down to the last centimetre. In a little while his breathing would become deeper and more regular as he slipped into a gentle doze, his moustache now being blown in and out with the rhythm of the air between his lips. He would always deny having been asleep and swear he had heard every word of our conversation. Admittedly at the end of an evening he could recount the plot of the radio play as well as tell you all about the book he had been reading, but perhaps that was another of his tall stories. His working trousers, not being made to measure, were always far too long, but he would tighten his braces and say they at least kept his chest warm. A pint of ale in the company of his family or friends was a great pleasure to him. Everyone knew 'Jumbo' Muirhead and we were tickled when his old friends would call out 'Good-night my beauty' or 'My old darlin','' as we wandered home of an evening. These expressions seemed funny to us as children, but that was the way of things in the country.

A great royalist, he was nevertheless most embarrassing to accompany to the cinema as he always rushed out before the playing of the National Anthem. This was not through any sense of disloyalty. The film show at the local cinema was not a continuous performance but only one house each evening, which finished just before 10 or 10.30p.m. Last orders at the 'Ship' a few doors away were called about the same time, so you had to be sharp to 'get one in' before making your way home. We would be gathering ourselves together as 'The End' appeared on the screen, standing to attention prior to singing the National Anthem when ... Bang! ... would go grandfather's seat as he scuttled through the nearest side exit, leaving us watching the doors swinging to and fro behind him, and hoping no one else had noticed who had gone out.

We always had a good laugh at figures of speech which were all his own. He made a joke of excusing his grammatical errors by saying he had not been 'edifiducted' like the youngsters of 'today', and of course, he had not. His parents had to pay 2d. per week for his schooling and with others in the family he was in fact quite lucky to stay at school until he was 12.

During the course of each day he came and went, in and out of the old back gate. First to the allotment, and then the golf course to stand with other hopefuls to be taken on for a round. There were still plenty of 'gentlemen' who could afford to pay someone else to carry their clubs, and present a handsome tip at the finish if they had found your company convivial. Grandad appeared to be well liked. He never seemed to tell anyone where he was off to, just lifting his cap from the peg behind the door, but Nan always knew. I suppose she was used to his routine, but my sister always liked to be told and have him bid her 'goodbye'. However quietly he tried to slip away, her piping little voice would follow him down the passage, 'Where are you going Grandad? You haven't kissed Nan and said 'goodbye'. Goodbye Grandad, Goodbye!' His face would crinkle with a smile at her persistence and she would eventually get a 'Cheerio' from his retreating back.

Our grandmother had come from a completely different background. Her grandparents were a farming family at Hempstead, with whom she had lived for a time during her childhood. Once a year we spent a day of our holiday visiting the 'ancestral home' as we laughingly called it. This was the farmhouse, a photograph of which hung in pride of place on the dining room wall. It was a two-storey, double-fronted house under a tiled roof, a central front door with a window above. We loved to hear the romantic story of our great-grandmother who eloped from that very window. It had been arranged for her to marry a cousin, heir to a neighbouring farm, so uniting family and property. Great-grandmother, however, had other ideas. She had fallen in love and one night she slipped away with the man of her choice. They had three little girls, and I like to think she was happy in her decision, although I understand their father died when they were quite young and they eventually went back to the farm where they were brought up. Great-grandmother later re-married, changing her name back to her family name. Whether it was to the cousin she had originally spurned, I do not know, but she became a farmer's wife and lived to a good old age.

The farm at Hempstead had passed out of the family many years before we used to visit it, and thereby hangs another tale, if I could unearth it. We used to take the bus part of the way and then, armed with a picnic, would stroll along the quiet lanes in the August sunshine. Nan would tell us about the governess cart in which she and her sisters would trot to school and church; about her step-father who was a local lay-preacher, walking miles some Sundays to reach a little hamlet and preach in the old church. His surname was Jacobs and with his flowing white beard, he could have come straight out of the Bible he carried under his arm. My own mother remembers how she loved this gentle, pious man.

We must always have chosen a good day for this outing. I remember the warm sun, the breeze stirring the dust in the lanes, the high banks ablaze with dancing red poppies, and a lark climbing high into the blue sky, his sweet, trilling voice spreading over the fields. Lunch was taken by the side of a village pond. It was the first occasion I can remember seeing a dragonfly. They were darting hither and thither in the heavy August air, all shimmering fluorescent shades of blue and green. We would sit for a while, perhaps making poppy-dollies from the flowers we had picked from the banks. Carefully folding down the scarlet petals would expose the black centre, which made a perfect curly head; a piece of stiff grass set below and tied with a strong, supple grass formed the arms and held the 'skirt' in place. Half the stalk broken off and pushed into place for the legs and we had a pretty dancing doll, like a little gypsy.

Having expended all our childish energy at the start of the journey, we were now beginning to say 'How much further, Nan?' 'Are we nearly there?' The answer was always, 'Just round the next bend, my beauties, not much further!'

I don't know how many bends she kidded us round, but it kept us going, passed the old farm and on into the village, where we caught the bus home. This outing always set my mother reminiscing about her summer holidays as a child with her grandmother and grandfather Jacobs on a farm further west in the Norfolk countryside. She would help to lead the horse to the farm waggons, ride on its back to the fields and during harvest ride home again on top of the hay.

Grandmother Jacobs would bake all her own bread in what was nothing more than a hole in the wall, with a fire under. Not even a range was available to her. Twice a day she would pack a basket with cold tea, bread and cheese, or pies and shorties for the farm workers in the fields. My mother, dressed in her little red cape, would carry it out for their 'elevenses' and 'fourses'. 'Here come my little maid,' her grandfather would say as she staggered across the stubble, and would then sit in the shade and share their refreshment. Could ever food have tasted finer!

Happy Days

We had many outings during our four weeks stay. For the first two weeks, if we were on our own, life was quietly satisfying. It was spent revisiting our favourite spots, hours on the beach, playing with our cousins, and trying to teach ourselves to swim. An old rubber inner tube was a great prize, and we would happily paddle about, tipping each other in and out. Sunbeds and rubber dinghies were unheard of in our circles.

At low tide we spent many happy hours scrambling on the rocks and playing in and out of the old 'wreck'. This was the remains of the 'Fernebo', sunk by a mine in 1917. Half of it had drifted along towards Overstrand and at low water a few chunks of metal were still recognisable as the shape of a boat embedded in the sand. Our mother and uncle had been among the many hundreds on the beach that dreadful January afternoon, watching the desperate attempts to rescue the poor sailors. The scene was still vivid in their memories.

Then the day would come when our mother was due to arrive and although we did not really feel that we had missed her, it was suddenly terribly exciting to think we would soon see her again. The morning would be spent on the beach as usual, but we would be off home early, ready to go and meet the train. As we came out of the woods the station could be seen on the hill top, outlined against the sky, the afternoon train for London getting up steam. Better hurry, it would be awful if the train came in and we were not there.

A quick tidy and we were rushing up the slope on to the platform. Right to the end we would go, where it ran down level with the track. This was our limit, but we were within shouting distance of the signal box, and would be kept informed of any delays further up the line.

The turn-table was placed at one side of the yard and with luck an engine would be on it. Watching this manouevre would keep us amused during our waiting time and we were always much too early. How two men could turn a great giant of an engine like that around never ceased to amaze us.

The man in the signal box would come and wave to us. 'Who are you meeting to-day my darlin's?' 'She's just at the junction, won't be many minutes now.' Almost immediately we would spy a puff of smoke over the hedgerows as 'she' came chugging round the bend. Dancing up and down with excitement we would wait for the carriages to snake into the platform, searching for the familiar face. Once spotted, for an instant it was not so familiar, as we always forgot how brown our mother became in the summer, and she nearly always had a new hat. This was usually small and white with a little veil or sprig of flowers. We almost pulled her out of the carriage, clamouring for hugs and kisses and was Daddy all right?

Laughing and chattering as much as us she would gather her bags together and we would set off. 'Hello Peggy', 'Nice to see you again' would follow us down the road as she met familiar faces.

During the next week we would visit great aunts and cousins. A day was spent in Norwich 'doing the rounds' of the various relations. Morning coffee in one home, lunch at another and afternoon tea somewhere else. Our heads were in a whirl, but it was all a bit of a bore after the initial excitement of being kissed and exclaimed over, and how much we had grown! None of the houses were appropriate for children. No toys to play with; pianos which 'must not be touched' and we were expected to be 'seen and not heard.' All our aunts and great aunts were very kind to us and we enjoyed the cakes and biscuits, but it was the 'grown-up' talk which left us out in the cold. We were not sorry to get home again, put on our old clothes and get back to the serious business of enjoying ourselves.

Nan never came on the beach. She did not like it and I think was rather afraid of the sea. It was quite an achievement to get her to a show on the end of the pier. She would keep peering down at the water between the planks of the deck as though it would swallow her up.

Sometimes she would join us in Happy Valley, and laugh with us as we rolled down the slopes and make ourselves feel deliciously dizzy. Or she would sit and cheer on our games of cricket. On one occasion she had run all the way to the top of the cliffs with raincoats for us all when we had been caught on the beach in a heavy downpour, and another time the family were hailed, and on looking up saw her little figure standing there with a basket of flasks of tea and biscuits. She had thought we would like a picnic.

After breakfast each morning, we children were sent off out of the way, so that mothers and aunts could clear up, make beds and help prepare dinner. These activities were no doubt all spiced with a good gossip. The adults did not meet so frequently and there was a great deal of catching up with family news to be done.

We were expected to tidy our rooms and empty the slops. All water was carried upstairs in big china jugs and after washing in the wide china bowls we rinsed them round and emptied them into the white enamel pails, together with any chamber pots which had been put to use during the night. None of us would dare to use the outside toilet in the yard in the middle of the night! My young sister was the 'slops maid'; she would struggle down the stairs and into the back yard to empty the pail in the shallow drain under the scullery window.

These jobs satisfactorily carried out we were free to run along, but there was no bathing until the adults joined us. With our towels rolled under our arms we proceeded to collect the necessary implements for a morning on the beach. We had various buckets and spades, balls, bats and nets, but always we had to take the big metal spade. Most of the spades we had were of wood with small blades and a short handle, but this one was the size of a small shovel with a sharp cutting edge. It belonged to a cousin who was usually with us, but the spade always stood just outside the back door for the use of any of the grandchildren. It was long enough to clang and clank along the ground with our every step, and as we invariably ran around without shoes, I have always been amazed that we all grew up with a full complement of toes. It was marvellous to scrape along the side of the many flint stone walls. The blade bounced from one stone to the next with a most satisfying sound. On the way home we would be chasing our tennis balls down the hill, running them in the gutters, one of us dragging the spade behind them, clanging on the road surface, which was warm and sticky, in the heat of the sun, to the soles of our bare feet. It was too uncomfortable to put plimsoles on feet covered with damp sand, and much too tedious to spend precious minutes cleaning them. By the time we arrived home the sand would have dried and fallen off. We never bothered to inspect the soles of our feet, but then we were back in the sea before very long. Nan's sheets must have suffered; I don't remember doing much washing before bedtime, but as her youngest son had always said the fairies would wash him, we used the same excuse.

The yard under the dining room window always held a row of our buckets containing all the treasures we had 'rescued' from the beach the day before. Pretty stones and seaweed were easily disposed of, or used to border the paths and flowerbeds in the small garden, but very often we had shrimps and kiddywitches (tiny crabs) which we were very reluctantly persuaded would be much happier if we took them back to their pools.

This little yard was a picture with pots of many shades of fuschia plants ranged along the window sills, pink, red, cerise and white. They hung like tiny lanterns amongst the dark green of their leaves.

Opposite the back door, in the shade, was the nearest thing to a refrigerator which my grandmother ever had. This was her meat safe. It was a wooden 'hutch' with a fine mesh covered door, held shut with a wooden catch. Everything always tasted fresh and I don't recall any tummy upsets.

Cream honeysuckle and large pink and white country roses climbed the fence and covered the arch over the high step leading to the tiny back garden. This was three parts filled with grandad's shed, a real treasure trove. We always had to take care to shut the screen door in case any of his birds were loose. On top of all his other interests grandad also bred canaries. Beautiful bright yellow Norfolk canaries with black shining eyes. Their sweet voices would fill the afternoon air, as the sun streamed in the window and warmed their cages. These were kept spotlessly clean, and we would often find grandad in there changing seed, putting in fresh water or gently taking a bird out for inspection of beak and claws.

To do this he would hold it in his gnarled and knotted hands. During his childhood the index finger of one hand had been amputated; he always told us it was through messing about with the rollers of his mother's wringer, but this may only have been to serve as a warning against doing the same with the great mangle which stood outside. This did mean, however, that a little bird could be held snug and cosy in the space left by the lost finger.

Opposite the double row of cages was a work bench holding all manner of tools, many brought from his cobbler's shop. Pieces of leather and polish all added their own aroma to the warm atmosphere.

The outside lavatory was built as part of the house at the time when inside water closets were considered really rather unhygienic. A wooden door with a lift-up latch opened into quite a spacious area with the lavatory seat, like a large wooden box with a hole in it, built across one end. A small window allowed a little light to penetrate, but as this was covered on the inside with transparent red and green squared coloured paper and on the outside by the climbing rose, it was quite a dim interior. It did, however, have the refinement of a flushing cistern with chain, suspended high in the corner. Quite an effort for little folks to reach, sometimes necessitating clambering up onto the seat.

One cousin confessed in later years that she had hated 'granny's loo', but I found it a warm and comfortable place in the late afternoon sunshine, a good place to snatch five minutes to yourself, perhaps propped on the wide seat, back to the wall, with a good book for company. Although in those days you could spend a few minutes reading the toilet paper! No soft tissues then! We had little squares of newspaper, carefully cut and threaded on a string hanging from a hook in the wall. As we usually dashed here after our walk from the beach, still in our bathing costumes, the floor and seat were nearly always gritty with sand and pieces of seaweed.

Dinner, at mid-day, was the main meal of the day and then we traipsed back to the beach or played cricket in Happy Valley. If the tides were not to our liking we would wander around the town peering in the beautifully dressed shop windows, in those days full of good quality articles; china, glass, brass and copper ware. There were so many shops to hold our interest apart from those which sold beach equipment, balls and kites; there were many which specialised in miniature figures of china, brass or glass and with our noses pressed to the window panes we happily exclaimed over the dainty pieces, arguing over which we would buy had we the money.

Our pocket money coveted no more than a few sweets or three pennyworth of chips for supper, and perhaps a visit to the cinema. One summer we made some extra money picking blackcurrants. Each morning for a week we were loaded into the back of a farm lorry; Nan, our mother and a couple of aunts and cousins, and driven to a farm, where we joined other friends and neighbours and settled down to a day amongst the currant bushes. Our picking was somewhat haphazard, but we made an effort and then played 'he' and hide and seek around the rows. Our mothers worked hard and had quite nice fat purses by Friday afternoon.

We took tins of sandwiches and cakes for lunch, which we ate with our blue-stained, sticky fingers. The scent of blackcurrants was almost over-powering in the warm sun as they hung like miniature bunches of grapes from the thick branches. After lunch we filled our tins with currants to take home, whilst our mothers dutifully continued to fill the farmer's baskets. I assume this was the recognised 'perk' of the job, because everyone seemed to do it, and we were never stopped or questioned as we left each evening.

On reaching home the sorting, topping and tailing began immediately, and then we had jam, pies, puddings, tarts ... everything smelled of blackcurrants, and we must have looked like them that autumn. What flavour they had! Just the scent of a blackcurrant leaf takes me back to that summer when I earned a whole half-crown for my share of the work. I was very proud of my very first week's wages.

Tea was a simple meal of bread and butter with shrimps or paste or maybe just a tomato, with a sprinkle of vinegar. These were large, sweet and juicy, still warm from the sun where grandad had picked them from the garden. There was home-made jam and cake - nothing fancy, plain fruit cake or shorties. I recall during the war we had 'shop' jam. The ration was one pound per person per month. As we were with Nan for four weeks we each chose our own flavour and kept our own jar of jam. We guarded it jealously, marking the side into four sections to be sure we did not gobble it all up at once. Oh, the scraping and licking of spoons to get every smear before it was reluctantly agreed we could scrape no more. It was a practical way to make us appreciate that there was only so much to go round and 'when it's gone, it's gone!' as we heard so often.

A boiled egg was another war time treat. People in the country fared better then than those in town and we had a few more luxuries at holiday time, including a nice brown egg for tea. Even so the game was to see how many 'soldiers' could be consumed before the last of the yolk had been dipped away. Nan sat at the corner of the table, a large crusty loaf clasped to her bosom. Wielding the bread knife she would cut across the loaf, each slice dipping further into the centre, until she was almost scooping each slice out. Eventually she would get tired trying to keep the plate filled and we would get a 'choking-off hunk' to keep us quiet, as she levelled up the loaf. 'You children would eat bread and jam until you're hungry,' she would laugh at us.

The baker called several times each week, swinging up the passage with his huge wicker basket and tapping on the back door. 'How many to-day, Mrs. Muirhead?'

One memorable day she emptied his basket, taking the whole lot, amidst much laughter from the children crowding the window. I am sure we were competing against each other to eat all we could. After dinner that day we were still peckish, or so we said, and asked for bread and cheese, but as the baker had not yet called, the bread bin was empty. This was a catastrophe in our eyes and we crawled under the larder shelves to investigate. All we could find were a few stale crusts put by for the rabbits. Having consumed these we still insisted we were hungry. After all we were growing boys and girls. 'Well you will just have to wait until the baker comes,' said Nan. So we knelt in the old arm chair gazing out of the window like little starving waifs. The latch of the back gate lifted and the bread basket appeared first, followed by the astonished face of the baker as a great cheer greeted him. Nan laughed at the poor man's expression and commenced to empty his basket. 'Poor little things,' she scoffed, 'they've even robbed the rabbits to-day. You would think they had never had anything. I don't know what I'm going to do with them!'

Each evening we would play for an hour or so over the Goat Field and perhaps have a bag of chips to finish the day, then we would be shoo'd off to bed. We would protest all the way that we were not tired and besides the sun was still shining. Double summer-time made the evenings long and light, but it was really quite late enough for us.

We would be allowed to play cards or read for half-an-hour and then as the games became noisier, with somersaults on and off the beds, we would hear Nan's voice calling up the stairs 'Will you go to sleep now. Any more noise and I shall be up with my copper stick, and give your bottoms a good thacking!'

We never got our hiding and giggling together we would settle down at last, and after a few moments listening to the sqeak of the rusty swings as the older children played, we soon fell into the deep satisying sleep experienced after hours spent in the bracing fresh, Norfolk air.

Family, Friends and Neighbours

 At odd times during the day, neighbours might pop in and out, just to say 'Hello, how are you?'; discuss the current news on 'the Park' and perhaps pick up a knitting pattern or recipe. Newspapers were exchanged every two or three days. I do not know who bought which, but we were often asked to 'pop these along to Mrs. Crane,' and would then be given two or three other papers together with a copy of 'Woman's Weekly' or the parish magazine to bring back. I enjoyed these papers and magazines; we did not have them at home, and I eagerly followed the adventures of 'Garth' and 'Jane' in the strip cartoons, and enjoyed the stories of a family of blackbirds in the magazines.

Nothing was ever discarded if it could be of further use to a neighbour. Even a bowl of soapy water was passed on. Somehow the water was hardly dirty after 'dinging out' a few woollies or undies, so Nan would pop along the passage, round the back gardens, her sleeves still rolled above the elbows. 'Thought you could use a drop of soapy water', she would say as she put the steaming bowl onto the draining board, 'I've only rinsed a couple of things out'.

We enjoyed running errands to the neighbours along the passage. They were always pleased to see us and find time to talk for a few minutes and sometimes give us a sugary biscuit. Mrs. Crane's home was a little more modern than Number 9 - she was younger than Nan - but still a homely, slightly untidy place. She had children in their late teens at this time. In fact, horrible little kids that we were, we used to spy on her daughter who was courting a local lad, and torment the life out of the pair. The romance still flourished, however, and perhaps we even added a little spice.

Old Martha and her sister seemed very ancient and terribly old fashioned, as was their home. It was dark, with heavy furniture and thick green velvet curtains and drapes. There were covers on everything, including the mantleshelf. They were tall, masculine women, with deep voices and thick lensed glasses. Their dark, heavy skirts, covered by faded voluminous overalls, fell to ankles encased in black leather boots tied with long laces or many little buttons. We were a little afraid of them, completely without cause, but also fascinated by their slow, rich Norfolk voices.

Mrs. Ringer, poor soul, lived on the opposite side of the passageway. and suffered all the noise and inconvenience of our comings and goings. Hardly ever did we run up the road home without one of us jumping on or over her low front wall. No harm was done or plants trodden on but we knew that it, quite rightly, annoyed her and of course did it all the more. She was a fussy, fastidious little woman continually looking for something about which to complain, or sitting behind her front lace curtains looking for someone to talk about.

Our grandmother had little time for her and her clinically clean home. She chided us when necessary but felt children would be children and must be given a bit of freedom. Mrs. Ringer had never had any children and was probably a lonely old lady with very little else to do except clean the house, and not a little envious of our grandmother's full and happy household. Our antics may have been a welcome diversion.

We were just as welcome to go and visit her as any of the other neighbours, and we would wonder how her long-suffering husband could stand her obsession with polish and whitewash. They were completely opposite in looks and temperament and therefore were, I suppose, compatible in their own way. 'Fred' was a large shambling man with a thick drooping moustache. His ill-fitting guard's uniform of navy serge making him appear even larger and shabbier. He smoked an old briar pipe with a bowl which must have held half an ounce of his strong, sweet tobacco. He would amble up the passage wearing his peaked cap, his green flag under his arm and his lantern hanging from one hand. He would pat us on the head with the other, a quiet smile creasing his kind eyes. It was 'common knowledge' that his slippers would be waiting for him outside the back door and if he wanted to have a smoke he must sit in the outside toilet.

His wife was a bird-like creature, all skin and bone, iron grey curls neatly framing her pointed little face, small round steel-rimmed spectacles perched on her nose. Her voice was high pitched, with a sing-song tone like a cracked bell. She never showed much annoyance towards us, but would come and twitter that we really should stop playing in the passage and wasn't it past our bedtime.

Their neat little garden was bordered with flint stones all painted white and regularly scrubbed or re-painted. The coal bunker, I am told, was emptied out each summer and white-washed!

We were once taken on a tour of inspection. I do not know why she thought two little girls would wish to look over her house, but it was such a contrast to our grandmother's cosy, untidy rooms, we could hardly believe we were in the same street. Everything gleamed with polish; tables, chairs, sideboards, mantleshelves, what-nots and aspidestras. The floor was like glass and with rugs scattered about its shining surface, it was as dangerous as walking on an ice-rink. The range was glossy with black leading so that you could see your face in it. It was obviously not used for any cooking as was ours. Upstairs was more spacious than Number 9, because they had the extra width over the passageway. We felt this was most unfair, there being only two of them and all that room!

When we took our leave she gave us each a large spoonful of cod liver oil and malt, of which we happened to be very fond. It made a good substitute for sweets, and we went happily home, licking our lips. Our mother, however, was highly indignant, feeling that Mrs. Ringer was under the impression we needed building up because we came down from London. We were told not to accept malt from her again, which we felt was a great pity as it tasted as good as toffee any day.

Two families of aunts and uncles still lived in or around Cromer and one or another would often call in for a cup of tea and a chat. Our cousins would always look in to get their pocket money or a sweet, shyly smiling at us until we all gradually fell back into the easy friendship and comradeship of previous holidays.

Our mother's oldest sister had been the last in the family to marry. Her husband was a regular soldier who after the war settled down as chauffeur and handyman for one of the large country estates a few miles outside Cromer. Public transport to and from the various cottages they lived in was next to non-existent and they would cycle over two or three times a week. Auntie had no sense of balance and was terrified on a cycle of her own, so uncle bought a tandem and she would pedal the miles away, perched on the back, quite happily.

Theirs was the only family wedding in which we had participated. My sister, only eighteen months old, was not at all happy to have her photograph taken and the records show a very miserable little girl with tearstained cheeks.

At four and a half I was very proud to be a bridesmaid for the first time, with two older cousins. We wore long, dainty cream cotton dresses, covered with tiny printed pink rosebuds, and each carried a posy of multi-coloured sweet peas. That is the extent of my memory of the day. Grandad grew all the flowers and the sitting room hearth was full of buckets and jugs containing bunches and bunches of these gorgeous blooms. They were like huge butterflies in every shade of pink, mauve, purple, cream and white.

They remained in the coolness of the front room until we were almost ready to leave for the church. I remember being handed my posy, the stalks wrapped in silver paper, but still dripping with water. To this day, whenever I smell the heady perfume of a sweet pea I can feel once more the damp stalks held tightly in my hot, sticky little hands.

During each holiday we would go to spend a day at whichever cottage our aunt and uncle were occupying at the time. Always it was a 'bus ride away. on a route which probably had only two or three 'buses a week.

We would alight at a cross-roads miles from any village and then walk what seemed to be about three miles along a narrow lane and 'just around the next bend' would be a pair of cottages set usually on the edge of a small wood. An idyllic setting on a beautiful summer's day, the winters must have been a trial. The sanitary arrangements were always extremely primitive, a wooden hut positioned at the far end of the garden. A deep breath was taken and held before reaching the door, whilst rushing in and out as speedily as possible.

We loved these tiny houses, with their low doorways and miniature windows. One had the front door almost permanently shut to keep out the frogs which insisted on hopping over the threshold. The staircase was almost always tucked behind a door in the kitchen, rising steeply to the bedroom. This would be built just under the eaves. On one occasion we tried to persuade our father to take the one next door. I do not know how we thought he would make a living as there were no factories just down the road, but it was a nice thought for a little while in the summer sunshine.

One year we had to travel by train for this visit. Nan took my sister and I, whilst our parents hired bicycles and enjoyed a spin together along the lanes. As we had a two hour wait for a connection on the way home, I think mum and dad had the quicker journey, as well as a good laugh. They stopped to enquire the way from an old man at the side of the road. 'Can you tell us the way to Honing?' He cupped his hand to his ear, then stroking his chin, whilst thinking deeply, he shook his head and replied 'Pony! No hen't seen one.' They had to hurry on their way to cover up their laughter and eventually arrived, still giggling like a couple of kids themselves.

We had cousins of all ages, some older, some younger. We enjoyed playing with the babies and taking them out in their prams. This particular aunt and uncle had a little boy latish in life, of whom we were all very fond. He was a dark, gentle little chap, with big brown eyes. He was not boisterous as a toddler, compared with the others, but loved to play games and be taken for walks. Sadly he was taken with cancer at three and a half years old, after a long, painful illness. As children we were devastated that such a thing should happen and felt so sad for our poor auntie who was unable to have any more children. We always stand for a moment by his little headstone and remember him when we visit the church at Overstrand where our parents, aunts and uncles were all married and where most of the grandchildren were taken 'home' to be baptised.

All Together Now

 Three weeks would go by happily and contentedly and we would suddenly realise that the next day our father would be coming for the final week of our holiday. Our joy was complete then, to see him after so long, with so much to tell, and we also knew that all the best outings and treats were being saved until he was with us.

Once again we were up at the station well before the train was due, chatting to the signalman and watching anxiously for the first puff of smoke. All at once the waiting was over and dad was climbing down onto the platform, trying to kiss and hug all three of us at the same time. 'Daddy I can swim!' 'Daddy I won at putting!' 'Daddy can we go in a boat this week?' We clamoured for his attention and he laughingly said 'Good' 'Yes' 'We'll see!' and we dragged him along, letting him know what was waiting for his dinner.

One year I met him with the question 'Did you find my balloon?' He looked at my mother mystified, not knowing what reply was expected of him, until we explained. The previous Saturday we had attended a fete at Northrepps Hall. It was a beautiful day and the grounds of the Hall were full of people in colourful summer dresses and hats and children running on the soft green lawns. Bunting hung from the trees and around the stalls and sideshows. The old Hall stood looking down upon us, homely with its large chimneys and ivy-clad walls. I can remember playing in a wooden rocking boat with my cousins, and which only recently I came across in a photograph in a book called 'The Northrepps Grandchildren', showing two or three little ones enjoying the same pleasure. There was also a 'balloon man' selling huge coloured globes filled with gas which kept them high in the air, straining at the limit of their strings, filling the summer afternoon with more colour as they bobbed along above the heads of noisy, happy crowds. We were all admonished to 'Hold on tight or you'll lose it!' which, of course, is precisely what I did. I was heartbroken as I saw my gorgeous balloon rising high into the sky and floating off into the blue. I was mollified by Nan saying 'Never you mind, my beauty, that will probably float all the way home to your daddy!' I consoled myself with this lovely idea and when everyone else had forgotten the incident, it was the first thing on my mind when greeting my father. I cannot remember the answer he gave me. I was either satisfied with it, or too excited and pleased to see him again for the matter to continue to be of such importance.

Our father's was not an extrovert personality, but he enjoyed his visits to the home of his mother-in-law so much, he was relaxed and content and became quite boisterous and school-boyish. This side of him first became apparent as he entered the passage and called 'Pour it out!' at the top of his voice, so that Nan would have his favourite cup of tea on the table. She was always called 'Emmie' by the in-laws. It was not her name, and I never enquired how she acquired it, but it suited her.

He always said that our holidays by the sea saved him a pile of doctor's bills. He swore we were set up for the the winter with the good food and fresh air; whenever a member of the family had suffered an illness of any sort, which fortunately was not often, we were packed off for Nan to 'build us up' again. She would have made a great nurse. Over the years, I suppose, she had plenty of practice with a large family, and she was always on hand at each confinement in the family.

Now our days were really full as we swam together, played putting, went to the pictures or a show on the pier. Games of cricket were organised, or disorganised, on the beach when the tide was out, or in Happy Valley. We laughed at our unfortunate aunts who tried so hard, but really were not up to batting and running after balls. We scoffed when they failed to make a simple catch and cheered on our fathers who were in their glory, running around like two-year-olds. They all soon lost their London pallor and seemed to grow younger and more handsome with each day that passed.

The path down the cliff to the beach was really no more than a sandy track between the gorse bushes. There were a few steep steps and then a wide path of loose sand and shingle going straight down. This was fine going down; you just took long strides, sinking into the sand with each step, and gathering speed the further you went, until you landed in a heap at the bottom. If you kept your footing and your legs could keep up with you, you eventually reached the beach and your headlong run was stopped as you levelled up and came to the water's edge - if the tide was in.

Coming back up was a different story altogether. What a drag to get back up that path! Three steps forward and two back, up to your knees in deep yellow sand, damp towels trailing, buckets and spades banging against your shins, a sharp stone catching between bare toes. It was worse with shoes as they soon filled up with sand and made climbing even more uncomfortable. Our mothers puffed and panted alongside us, the menfolk cracking jokes and making matters worse as the ladies laughed and giggled so much that they eventually fell over. One uncle, trained in the London Fire Service during the Blitz, amazed us all one day by picking up his wife, throwing her over his shoulder and giving her a fireman's lift to the top. How his legs got him there we never knew, but it put us all to shame.

A day was usually spent at Yarmouth and for once regular mealtimes were forgotten and we were allowed to eat and drink anything we fancied, whenever we felt like it. What a mixture! We wandered around the market sampling cockles and shrimps, then an ice cream, along the front for candy-floss and lemonade, a bag of chips and possibly a hot and sugary doughnut. A trip in a pony and trap, then on to the pleasure gardens, a few rides on the roundabouts, a spill down the helter skelter into the huge wooden bowl at the bottom, skirts flying, showing all auntie's bloomers and then the great thrill of a ride on the big dipper, for those brave enough to face it, usually children and dads. It was fantastic! I wondered why I felt faint when we got back!!!

The train took us home again, after an exciting day. We were almost too tired to walk from the station. Our chatter could no longer be heard as Nan ushered us home, leaving the 'grown-ups' to have a quiet drink at the Suffield Hotel.

For once we did not argue about bedtime. It was marvellous to slide between cool, lavender-smelling sheets. The room was lit at regular intervals as the beam from the lighthouse swept round and round. We counted the seconds between the flashes, but soon our heavy eyelids closed as we re-charged our batteries for another day.

One of our favourite outings was to the salt marshes at Blakeney. A day would be spent up to our knees in mud, gathering cockles, chasing each other in and out of the little pools, picking samphire and walking out at low tide towards the Point, until our only landmark was the twin towers of Blakeney church.

This was an exciting experience. The outgoing tide left fast-flowing channels of water which had to be forded. Sometimes the mud and sand became very soft and threatened to trap our legs, like quicksands. Even on the warmest day a fresh breeze would blow across these marshes. With the tang of salt in the air, our faces would burn very quickly, though we had been exposed daily to sun and sea air.

We always took a couple of sacks with us because there was a serious side to this outing. We were all very fond of cockles for tea and here they were to be had for nothing more than the trouble of picking them up. Sometimes they spat at us as they closed their shells tight and endeavoured to sink back into the mud.

By the water's edge, amongst the many plants peculiar to the salt marshes and in the dozens of pools dotted about the shore, grew the seaweed-type plant called samphire. We looked upon it as the poor man's asparagus.

Our grandmother would have the copper boiling or tin baths on the gas stove, one for the cockles and one for the samphire. After washing off the loose mud they would be tipped in and boiled; then, still steaming, lifted onto the table in great soup tureens. We all helped ourselves, adding vinegar and pepper to enhance the flavour. Soon only a heap of shells and a dish full of stalks remained and we had had a meal fit for a king. Some of the samphire was pickled in jars to enjoy during the winter with cold meat or fish.

On one occasion I wonder we were able to get our sacks full of treasure home. It was a good bus ride from Blakeney to Cromer and unfortunately the afternoon had turned to a drizzly rain. We had gathered all we could and decided to call it a day. Normally we would bathe and clean ourselves of the caked-on mud, but on this day we were not only muddy, but also wet and cold. To make matters worse we had with us a large springer spaniel who had enjoyed his day as much, if not more than, the rest of us. We all piled into the bus, making for the rear seats, to be as inconspicuous as possible. A mixed group of adults and children, two muddy sacks and a large, bedraggled dog, who in the warmth of the bus soon began to smell to high heaven. We felt quite ashamed when the conductor came for our fares, and were sure that he would turn us off. My mother swore she would never take 'that animal' to Blakeney again.

We all loved Santa dearly. He was my mother's brother's dog and always seemed to be a part of our holidays, trotting along with us, playing on the beach, and running up and down the cliffs. I don't remember him ever being on a lead. He lived until he was at least sixteen so it is no wonder that he always seemed to be present; his life span covered all our early memories.

Soon the days were speeding fast to the end of our month. We might fit in a day on the Broads. No cabin cruisers or motor launches; we hired a rowing boat for a day and taking a picnic lunch we would glide along what were then the quiet waterways, hands trailing in the soft, cool water. We watched the sparkling droplets fall from our fingers, fed the many water birds and admired the wooden bungalows set at intervals along the banks, each with its own mooring point where the lawns swept down to the water's edge.

Our father worked hard but seemed to enjoy the steady rhythm of dipping and pulling on the oars with his strong arms, the golden hairs gleaming in the sun. He had taught me to row, and on one of these outings I used all my strength and determination to prove myself worthy of his teaching. After all he had been a merchant seaman and loved everything connected with the sea. I rowed the full length of Wroxham Broad with a full boat. The wind was getting up as the afternoon turned towards evening, but I refused to give up my oars until I had completed the course. My arms ached, but I was well satisfied with my achievement.

We spent many happy hours one holiday composing a family song. Everywhere we went we chanted, tried out new phrases, extended them to form a verse, bringing in the chorus each time, until we nearly drove our grandmother out of her wits. Her youngest son and his family were due to arrive and we were being hurried out of the house in order that she might get a bit of tidying-up done before they came. Normally she said 'The place was cleaned before you came, and I shall give it a good 'fie-out' after you have gone.' So we had to pull her leg about doing extra housework in the middle of our holidays, just because her 'favourite' was coming. One of the other uncles, a son-in-law, started the joke. He loved to tease her and tried to get her going on many discussions, but Nan was a good match for him. Religion, politics, unions, she always had an opinion to voice and a well-thought-out argument. We were too young to take in the details of their discussions but Nan always appeared to be well-read and fair-minded in her conclusions.

On this occasion, however, uncle was not letting her off. 'Just because her favourite little boy is coming the house must be made spick and span. Bet she doesn't do it for us!' and he started off to the tune of 'The Quartermaster's Stores':

There was muck, muck, enough to fill a truck, On the floor, on the floor, There was muck, muck, blooming great piles of muck, At the Muirhead's boarding house.

This went on in rhyme to the effect that a great clearing-up was taking place because 'Her son, Reggie, is coming to stay.' We added verse after verse on various themes, each trying to cap the other with our wit. It gave us a great feeling of togetherness as we sang our song along the cliff tops. We had eventually all been swept out of the kitchen with the broom for being cheeky.

The same uncle instigated further hilarity one day when our mothers were whipping a synthetic cream for tea. Real cream was unheard of still, and a powdered form mixed with milk had been recommended for a treat. It came up very light and fluffy, and we were all sitting around the table after dinner watching this operation, when uncle in a very innocent voice wondered what would happen if you coughed or sneezed while lifting a spoonful to your mouth. Naturally we children dared him to try, and without much persuasion he did just that! The effect can be guessed only too well! White fluffy dobs of cream flew around the room and across the table, whilst we shrieked with delight at this naughtiness. Grandmother was endeavouring not to laugh, our mothers were telling him what a terrible example he was to us all, and one aunt was disgusted with his childish action and sat stiff-backed and straight-faced, her lips compressed tightly together, every inch of her conveying disapproval. Unfortunately she did not know that a large blob had settled on top of her hair at the front of her head, turning her grim countenance into complete comedy, but she never did see the funny side of it, and could not understand why our laughter was increased.

We had a great deal of make-do and synthetic foods, until the real things were again available to us. Lemonade was made from lemon essence and hot water. It always seemed to be warm, as there was no ice or refrigerator in the ordinary home, and the oil always floated on top, making bottles and glasses greasy. I suppose we were glad of it to quench our thirst, as a change from plain water.

Blancmanges and milk drinks were coloured and flavoured with various essences. De Carls was a trade name for many colourings which contained flavours very close to the real fruit. As we were unable to purchase these at home, our suitcases on our return always contained a box of little coloured bottles, enough flavours to keep us going for a few months in milk shakes, or for colouring sugar when icing sugar was like gold-dust.

In the country eggs were easier to come by and any surplus, I remember, were preserved in buckets of water containing isinglass. This formed a light, soapy film on top and we were dared to touch it as this would allow the air to enter and the eggs would go off. I was fascinated by this process and one day could not resist creeping into the back bedroom where the buckets were stored under the wash stand and just running my finger across the opaque film floating on the surface. I was terrified for weeks that I would be the cause of wasting a bucketful of precious eggs in those hard times, but I never heard that there had been a disaster in that direction.

Homely Fun

Evenings were the time for genteel walks in the country. We put on dresses, clean socks and shoes and brushed our hair. This, by now, was getting very sticky and tangled, our scalps full of sand. We were supposed to brush and comb it out each morning and Nan would help us re-plait and tie the ribbons at the end. We both had hair that was almost long enough to sit on, but it was such a nuisance and if no one noticed we just tidied the top so the knots above our ears, where we were continually pushing back loose ends, got worse and worse. Woe betide if Nan caught us! Out came the rubber padded brush with its steel prongs and, hopping from one foot to the other, we were sorted out. 'Will you stand still! The more you hop the worse it will be!' All the burrs we had thrown at each other were tugged out and brushed away and we were eventually released.

When we were suitably tidy we would stroll up 'Bunny Curtis' hill in the shade of the trees, or along the Avenue, past Northrepps Hall, where our mother and her brother had been chased many a time by the gamekeeper when they were children in case they disturbed the pheasants on their eggs. They did find a cluster once and gleefully, in all innocence, took them home to their mother, as they would a bunch of wild flowers. They thought they were a sort of potato. She, of course, realised the seriousness of this action and insisted they took them straight back and replaced them. Whether they ever hatched out is doubtful, but the children were fortunate not to be caught. This young brother was always threatening to run away and eat turnips if he did not get his way, and one day actually carried out this threat, but he only went as far as the Goat Field, where he could be sure he would soon be found.

We would gather wild strawberries from the banks and sometimes pull bunches of hogweed for grandad's rabbits. This was a great delicacy for them and we were proud to help in their care.

We thrilled to the idea of walking past the 'haunted house'. It looked like any other large old house in the district, but locally was always called haunted and you never knew, you might just see something ghostly if you looked hard enough! This legend had grown up during the infamous years of smuggling on the Norfolk coast, when they needed to keep ordinary folks out of the way and to account for any strange lights or noises which might be seen or heard during the night. A monster dog was reputed to roam one of the back lanes and no one dare venture there after dark.

As we grew older going for a walk became a bit of a bore which we tried to get out of. In fact I did more or less refuse one evening and was told I could stay in providing I cleaned the fish forks and knives, which form of punishment I perversely rather enjoyed, apart from the fact that grandad and I scared the life out of each other because we both thought we were alone in the house. Each thought the other was a burglar!

However, if we took the lane past the haunted house we knew we were in for a pleasant evening, although a long walk, and a late night for us. We continued on our way past another old country house with a concealed driveway. To assist vehicles entering the road a large speckled mirror was placed on the opposite bank. We would spend a few minutes pulling weird faces at ourselves, made more horrible by the convex surface of the glass. It was as good as the hall of mirrors at a fairground. On round the winding lanes to the next village of Northrepps to pay a visit to the Foundry Arms, a favourite little drinking house of the family. We, of course, had to remain outside, but there was a pleasant yard, with chickens and cats to play with and we usually had a ball to bounce around.

Peering in at the low doorway we had an impression of dark beams and gleaming brass, and a large chimney-breast with a brass fender around the hearth. There was a room full of small tables and chairs with lace table centres and vases of flowers. It looked so cosy, like someone's sitting room, genuine olde-worlde, and we were peeved not be included in the party. We were given a large glass of fizzy lemonade, one between two, with straws. 'Not one each?' We were insulted at having to share, but it was such a large glass, we could not in all honesty have managed one each. As it was, we were burping all the way home.

If it was late and we were getting tired a happy evening out was crowned with a ride home on the bus. Nan's legs had had enough so she would shepherd us all home. We waited for the little red single-decker in the yard of the Foundry Arms, our mothers and fathers setting off to enjoy their walk back in the cool of the evening. The bus came meandering through the lanes, chugging along in the twilight. We scrambled on board, clambering onto the high side seats - much to Nan's discomfort - the better to look out for, and wave to, the walking party as we passed them somewhere along the way. Before they arrived home we would be safely in our beds.

Sunday evening particularly we were expected to be more sedate in our behaviour. In fact I don't think we went to the beach so much on Sundays. Even if we did not go to church or Sunday school there was a certain difference about Sunday. On would go our 'best' dresses and we would all stroll gently into the town. Our father always liked to savour a walk and his normal stride was slowed to a measured tread. No amount of tugging at his arm and 'Let's go a bit faster, Dad,' would alter his pace. He had to work to the clock all the year, so now he took his own time. Our grandparents smiled and nodded to friends and neighbours, proud to be out with their family.

We wound our way through the pathways in North Lodge Park, flanked by the many formal flower beds which surrounded the putting greens, kept immaculate by the gardeners. Each bed was a blaze of colour set amongst the neatly shorn lawns, with every year a different colour scheme and sometimes an emblem picked out with corresponding coloured plants, a small work of art.

Along past the bowling greens. Sunday evening was favourite for this gentle form of sport, and we would stand a while, ranged along the railings with other spectators, admiring the skill of the, mostly elderly, gentlemen enjoying a friendly competition. There always seemed to be a 'Herbert' among the players and we smiled at the encouraging comments of the team leader. 'Come you round this side a bit 'Harbut'! Tha's the way, lovely wood...beautiful!!'

And so on through the town and down to the front. There were no chips to-night. No fish and chip shop would dream of opening on a Sunday night, but a favourite call of our elders was to the Bath Hotel along the promenade. This was the old 'Bath House' when people bathed in the salt water for their health, before sea bathing became popular. They had their baths and were then served refreshments. Later it was refurbished as a public house with a large pleasant lounge overlooking the sea-front. Furnished with pink and green basket chairs picked out with gold and cushioned with comfortable seats, scattered around glass topped tables, it was an elegant and companionable atmosphere to spend an evening. I believe there was even a small orchestra on occasions. Children left on the grass outside or on the beach could play in safety and a watchful eye be kept on them.

Being dressed for an evening out we were not expected to play in the water or with the sand, but would gather pebbles, chase each other up and down the many sets of steps and roll our ball along the promenade, daring it to go through the small holes left for drainage, onto the beach below.

One evening the tide was high up the beach and gradually creeping in to cover a long concrete slope. A wave would splash up to its edge and recede, then the next few would barely reach it. Suddenly one bolder than the rest would rush up and go a little further than the previous highest. We ran up and down from slope to beach watching the gradual encroachment of the sea. We could still get past without wetting our feet. As the tide rose the waves grew stronger and the force of the spray greater, hitting the wall before being sucked back. There was no danger; the water would not get very deep even when the tide was at its height. The fun was to dodge the spray as we tried to cross before the next wave covered the sand. With all the excitement and the warmth of our exertions we did not realise just how wet we were getting.

Suddenly Nan was standing at the head of the slope! 'What do you think you are doing? You are drenched to the skin. Now, do you run all the way home and get that wet dress off. You'll get the tick-dolly-roos!'

I looked down at my light mustard crepe-de-chine frock. It was wet from frilly neck to hem, a much darker colour and all crinkled and shrunk up, as crepe-de-chine does when wet. It was so tight I could hardly breathe, but I did run all the way home, my grandmother's threats ringing in my ears.

What were the 'tick-dolly-roos'? We were always going to catch them if we got wet or did not eat proper meals or forgot to take a woolly when the weather turned chilly. Many years later, looking through a medical dictionary, I came across the complaint ticdouloureux - a form of neuralgia with twitching of the face muscles. This I assume is the correct terminology for my grandmother's tick-dolly-roos. Where she acquired this phrase I have no idea and was extremely surprised it had any basis in fact; I thought it was a figment of Nan's imagination.

She was also very fond of telling us to 'cock up your leg and say sugar,' if she wanted a foot lifted off the ground for lace tying. Why did we have to say 'sugar'? It still remains a mystery.

Our meal times by now must have kept grandmother busy all day. We had hearty appetites but she rose to the occasion and we were never disappointed. Our mothers helped, of course, with the preparation and washing-up. The baker came regularly and also the milkman, and what a picturesque sight that was. No electric van loaded with plastic crates and rattling bottles. Mr.Stevens progressed slowly up the roads with his horse-drawn milk float. Three or four large churns stood in the body of the float and hanging round the outside were long-handled milk ladles, pint and half-pint measures. When we heard his pony clopping up the road Nan would take down a large, white, straight-sided jug from the shelf and ask us to pop out and get the required number of pints from Mr.Stevens. He would be positioned in the middle of the road, his horse quietly waiting, enjoying the fussing of the children, one or two ladies standing chatting, their white jugs held closely to them as they awaited their turn. Mr. Stevens would mount the step at the rear of the float, choose the appropriate measure and ladle out the thick creamy milk straight from the churn into the next waiting jug. I suppose there were flies about and plenty of dust on a summer's day but it was so much more romantic than having a standard shaped and sized bottle plonked on the step.

Finding room for us all to sit down to meals was a work of art. The four sides of the large square dining table were fully occupied by the 'grown-ups', so we children were elevated to the front room, where we had our very own table, laid up in the correct fashion with a full complement of cutlery and a cruet.

Our meal was served first and we were warned to 'Eat it all up and behave yourselves. No larking about in there!' We did not need telling twice to clear our plates, for everything was too good to waste. Having scraped the last smear of gravy we would look at each other 'Whose turn is it to ask for seconds?'

Poor little Maxie was the youngest and we always found some excuse for it to be his turn, either a forfeit he must pay or a punishment for some mild misdemeanour. He never held it against us, and, with a resigned sigh, would pick up his plate and advance slowly to the door, behind which our families were settling down to their own dinner. As the door knob rattled in his little hands we could hear them laugh 'Here they come!' and we all crowded in behind Maxie, our plates held before us like a lot of little Oliver Twists. 'Any seconds?' 'Please can we have some more?'

'Good gracious, have you eaten that already? We've hardly sat down. You'll have to wait a minute.' Nan always found us a little more and we would scuttle back to our table, well pleased with ourselves.

Our mother laughs now at the memory of our faces peering around the door, as they used to wait for our coming and the cry of 'Any seconds?'

Perhaps there would be one free day now to fit in a coach outing to finish off the week. On one occasion we visited Castle Acre, the ruins of an old priory. Auntie Gertie was in a frivolous mood all day, and kept us all laughing at her silly little jokes. We went on then to the Shrine of Our Lady of Walsingham, and the beautiful little Slipper Chapel, a couple of miles outside the village. Pilgrims, over the years, would leave their shoes here to walk barefoot to the Shrine. We climbed down from the coach eager to enter the chapel only to be informed that, it being a Roman Catholic place of worship, our heads must be covered. We looked at each other with disappointment, for not one of us had even a headscarf. Then auntie came to the rescue. Never one to be idle she had spent the journey busily employed with her crochet hook, making a set of table mats. They were off-white in colour, circular and made perfect little skull caps when placed demurely upon our heads.

In single file we entered the church, stifling the giggles which rose in our throats at the thought of the table mats perched on our heads. It was cool and sweet smelling inside with the masses of summer flowers, their perfume drawn out with the warmth from the dozens of candles flickering around the altars.

With due reverence we passed down the minute aisle, only to be convulsed with laughter as the silence was broken by the clang of metal on stone. One of us still had the crochet hook entwined in the cotton and of course it had loosened its hold and clattered to the ground. We had to beat a hasty retreat to the gardens, where we clutched each other, the tears rolling down our faces.

I hope no one present at the time thought badly of us or assumed we found our surroundings humourous. It was just the last straw in a day full of laughter and jokes peculiar to our own family. I have been to the Shrine on a few occasions since that time and it is as beautiful and peaceful as I remember. Full of the atmosphere of centuries of the worship of pilgrims; but always amongst the peace and quiet, I hear the tinkle of a crochet hook, as it slithers down someone's back to the floor. Now we were visting all our favourite spots to hold in the memory for another year. Having a last meal of crab, or cockles, Charlie's sausages, Creamola custard - Nan's was always the best tasting, although we also had it at home. One uncle would treat himself to a lobster and another night there was duck and green peas, a rare delicacy. So much so the meal was delayed until the evening, after the children were in bed, but not asleep, with the aroma of roast duck drifting up the stairs. We were most indignant at being excluded. We had never tasted duck! I don't imagine our parents had more than a taster each, as they had to make one duck go a long way, but it gave them all a lot of pleasure!

One year the uncles managed to round up a box of fireworks. This was a rare excitement. The back yard was too small for safety, so we all assembled on the goat field. It was still day light, but the long summer evening was drawing in slowly. Our fathers enjoyed themselves immensely, like a lot of school boys showing off to their friends. Half Suffield Park seemed to have arrived to see what all the excitement was about and a free firework show was not to be missed. I don't know the legalities of holding a private firework party in a public place, but no one interfered and we had a marvellous show. Nan sat, like a little queen, on a chair at the edge of the circle. Surrounded by neighbours, she proclaiming proudly that the entertainment was being provided by her sons and sons-in-law.

Goodbyes

 Saturday was fast approaching. Clothes were being gathered up from odd corners and thrown into the case. Shoes were rescued from under chests, plimsoles thrown into the dustbin - no point in carting those soggy relics home. Hair ribbons, hankies, socks all yellow with sand. Socks could be boiled in those days and they certainly needed it.

Saturday morning! A last run up through the woods, walk along the wall, run into Happy Valley and then to the top of the cliffs. Bye-Bye beach, bye water, bye pier, see you next year.

Back to Nan's, using as many favourite paths as possible, a last pebble down the well, make a ball like a little hedgehog of burrs to take home, and then an early lunch.

Cases were packed and rackets re-strapped to the outside. 'Now are you sure you've got everything?' The house began to look bare without all our paraphernalia lying around. 'Time's getting on. You'd best be getting on up that there hill,' Nan urged us in to action.

Grandad would hump our cases onto his old 'barra' and with the dads would start off ahead of us, pushing it up the long slope to the station. Reluctantly we would follow, turning to gaze up at the lighthouse and take a last glimpse of Number 9, the corner shop and the fish and chip shop. Tonight we would not be joining the queue for our three pen'orth of chips in newspaper. We would be back in Hornchurch where it would be warm and sultry after the fresh breezes from the sea, the house stuffy after being shut up for a couple of weeks.

The train usually stood in the platform for about twenty minutes before departure time and we settled ourselves and our luggage in good time. Standing on the platform we passed the time of day with neighbours and friends on their way to Norwich for a shopping trip. 'Off again then, had a good holiday? See you next year.'

The engine, either fresh from the sheds or puffing round the loop from Sheringham, was coupled on and the guard, busily supervising the loading of parcels and mail, hurried past. His green flag would be at the ready. It might be kindly Fred Ringer, from next door, to give us a warm smile and a pat on the head. 'She'll soon be off, my darlin's, best be getting in!'

Warm hugs and kisses were exchanged all round, as with lumps in our throats and smarting eyes, we climbed aboard. ' Bye Nan, bye Grandad. See you soon!' Green flag waving, 'Right away' from the guard, an answering toot-toot from the engine and we slowly started our long journey home. There was a last glimpse of the sea beyond our grandparents. We waved frantically before sliding round the bend. The watertower and lighthouse were seen briefly through a blur of tears. 'Why do we have to go home?' Our mother, too, was quiet for a while, as she did not see her parents very often; but then we cheered ourselves up. It would be nice to see our friends again, and although September meant back to school we also had our birthdays to look forward to, and a big party.

September was the month for mine and my father's birthday, on the same day, and then our grandmother's, followed by my sister's. Usually Nan and grandad came to spend a few days with us before autumn and winter set in. They came separately, as someone had to feed and clean the rabbits each day. So perhaps it wasn't too bad!

It was cosy to be travelling all together now, with so much to talk about, or just to dream at the window. The fields had all been harvested, and the gold of early August had given way to the dull, dryness of early September. The sky was still blue but there was a freshness in the air and the days were growing shorter.

Liverpool Street was just as busy and dirty. People scurried about, but the anticipation and excitement had left us. 'How long before our train goes?' The cases would be heavy and we thirsty. 'Won't be long now, there's a fast train to Romford, and then we'll get a taxi and be home in no time!' This rare treat was the final excitement of the holiday.

At last we were drawing up to our own front gate. How overgrown the garden looked. Dad was anxious to get lawn mower out and start tidying up. Our mother must be thinking of all those grubby, sand and grass stained clothes to be washed, and school outfits to be sorted out for the next week. But first a cup of tea and something to eat. 'Who wants a Charlie's sausage for tea?'

How quiet the house, until after tea we sit and watch our father wind and re-set the Westminster chiming clock on the bureau. Patiently and gently he moves the hands from one quarter-hour to the next, allowing it to chime fully before moving on. So the hush of the house is enlivened by the many chimes as he brings it around to tell the correct time once more. The familiar tick brings us slowly down to earth and back to our usual routine. A good night's sleep in our own soft feather bed will soothe away the sadness in our hearts, and tomorrow everything will seem normal again!

Other Times

 On a few occasions we visited our grandparents between summer holidays. Once or twice we spent Christmas with them. I remember our concern as to whether Father Christmas would know where to find us and whether he would be able to get down Nan's chimney? Her fireplace was much smaller than the one in our sitting room at home. We need not have worried. I can remember waking on Christmas morning to the sight of two bulging pillow cases, one with a teddy bear peeping out at the top. My sister has him to this day, with renewed pads on his paws, and a good deal less fur!!

A later year I had my first pair of fur gloves, a real grown-up luxury. I also had a poisoned thumb and had great difficulty pulling on the gloves over the bandage. It was a crisp, sparkling, Christmas; the sky as blue as summer, but the air sharp with frost, stinging eyes and nose. I was proud to walk out with my new gloves in spite of the pain. I had pulled at a loose cuticle and must have got some dirt in it, and by the time we got to Cromer it was red and angry-looking. Nan was a great poultice maker, and soon had me dipping it in near boiling water. Then I was wrapped up in a poultice of bread soaked in boiling water and told 'not to make such a fuss' as I squirmed away from her administrations. It was agonising but it 'drew' the poison to such an extent I had to visit the doctor to have the finger lanced. I have often wondered since whether a poultice draws more poison than is there in the first place. Would these small eruptions have healed more quickly if left alone?

It was seldom I saw a doctor and half the few occasions seemed to be at Cromer. It became quite a joke that I had a crush on one of the local doctors. Each year I came out in a rash of heat spots, great itchy things. The only respite was to dab them with vinegar, as nothing else soothed it. I would climb the stairs each night with my little saucer and a piece of cotton wool. By the morning I smelled like a fish and chip shop.

Nan eventually carted me off to the doctor as this was happening every summer. He diagnosed over-heated blood through sheer excitement contained inwardly instead of letting off steam (and driving everyone else mad). Nothing to be done about it! I grew out of it.

Another year a cyst grew on my eye-lid which again necessitated a visit to the doctor's lance. That was not pleasant, and I was glad when it was all over, but I was rather proud of my bandage swathed head, for a little while!!

Our father always felt Number 9 was the best convalescent home you could wish for; as a baby I had been very poorly after a comparatively minor operation, but a short stay had soon perked me up again. So when he had a very serious cycle accident, having been knocked down one foggy night by a motor cycle, it was the place he chose to regain his strength. He had been told at first that he would not walk again, and then, after he had proved that he was determined to regain the strength in his legs, that he would never be without a limp. Certainly, after many weeks in hospital he did not look as though he would ever be able to do more than hobble. We saw him for the first time, tall, pale, his flesh fallen away. He clasped a walking stick with one hand and tried not to lean too hard on our mother's arm, as he endeavoured to greet us with a smile.

I don't remember how long we were away but he came back strong, smiling, walking straight and tall and fit for work once more at his bench in the factory, where he was a sheet metal worker.

I do remember that it was spring time, the woods were carpeted with bluebells and primroses, the sun sparkling through the trees. Later the rhododendrons gave their usual magnificent display around the woods of Northrepps Cottage and down our favourite 'dark lane'. Exotic blooms in every shade from deep red through the pale and dark mauves to richest purple, painting the countryside with colour set against the dark, dark green of their huge shimmering leaves. We loved to shuffle and scuff our way down this quiet lane. Traffic was virtually non-existent in this back-water. The woods stood high above us, the banks either side taller than we were, the upper branches of the trees bending to entwine, blotting out the sky. The dank, damp smell of rotting leaves greeted our nostrils as we waded through the piles lining the edge of the bank. Sometimes these were knee deep and we screamed and shrieked with laughter as we endeavoured to push each other over, falling into the soft mounds, sometimes to be covered completely.

We were so happy to be enjoying this extra holiday and sorry for our school mates tied to their desks. Our mother suggested we pick some flowers and send them a breath of country air. So a box of exquisite primroses, packed in moss, was duly parcelled up and posted direct to our junior school.

A short time later we received a small package, addressed to me, and inside was a bundle of 'thankyou' letters, one from each member of the class. Our teacher had used the primroses as a writing exercise. Each letter was correctly set out and addressed and each one in its own way told us exactly the same news. I still have that bundle and the individual characters come to life in the way that each person expresses themself with the same information.

After thanking us for the flowers, and saying how beautiful they look in bowls around the classroom, we hear about the latest school activities and particularly about the Book Drive, as well as who had measles or mumps.

This was still wartime and children were being encouraged to collect books of every size, shape and form. I assume they were to be pulped down and recycled for paper and cardboard. There was great rivalry amongst the avid collectors, because each bundle or number of books entitled you to a badge proclaiming your status in the 'Waste Paper Army!' So many for a private, then on to a corporal, sergeant, captain, and, I believe, major, the coveted top rank.

I had been at school during the launch of the campaign, but our father's illness had taken us away before we had a chance to rise in the ranks. Our friends letters gave us full details of everyone's position, particularly the boys, who must have combed the streets daily, begging books from all and sundry, so that they might wear with pride the cardboard circle proclaiming them to be captains in the Book Drive.

I can see us all sitting around the dining room table, passing the letters among us, reading out little bits and pieces to each other, laughing over the style or spelling of some choice remark. There must have been thirty or forty letters in that bundle and by the time we had been through them all we certainly knew, well and truly, what had been taking place at Park Lane School during our absence. Although we laughed at the repetition we were deeply touched that such an effort had been made by way of thank s for a box of primroses.

My father's convalescence was not the only one taken in Cromer at that time. On every walk we came across not only soldiers training and preparing themselves for action overseas, but also those who had already been and had returned to receive hospital treatment, operations and then weeks or months of rest. We met them everywhere, dressed in their bright blue hospital uniforms, on crutches or walking sticks, legs in plaster, arms in slings, shoulders on metal braces. They hobbled around the town or sat in the sunshine on the seats outside the Leicester Home at Overstrand, the length of the drive from the house probably being as far as some of their legs could carry them. They would smoke a cigarette and pass the time of day sitting either side of the wrought iron gates, before making their way gently back again.

The hospital seemed to have its fair share of military patients. One ward at the side had been built to nurse T.B. patients, and the whole of one wall consisted of sliding and folding glass doors, through which they could benefit from all the sunshine available. In good weather the doors were thrown open to let the fresh air do its healing work. I don't know whether the men we saw during the war were T.B. cases or orthopaedic, but on our way to the beach we could look over the hedge at the rows of beds in the sunshine, some with pulleys, some with bed-cradles. We thought it look most peculiar, men in striped pyjamas lying in their beds 'outside'. We always waved to them as we skipped by and received many a cheery greeting in return.

About this time we were introduced to the now elderly lady who had been our mother's teacher when she had been about our age. She was delighted to see us all and smiled as she said, 'Peggy, you were never much of a scholar, always looking for some mischief, but you were never really naughty, just full of fun, and you always were a good reader!'

If this lady had not been able to teach her a great deal at least she instilled in her a love of literature and poetry. Many poems had been learned by heart and never, to this day, forgotten. Hiawatha and The Legend of St. Christopher are two which, even now, with a little thought, she can bring to mind. She would stand on the cliff top, the breeze whipping her skirts around her knees, head high, hair streaming back and throwing her arms wide would recite,

The sea, the sea, the open sea,

The great, the wide, the ever free.

Without a mark, without a bound,

It runneth the earth's wide regions around.

The teacher at the little village school did her job well for the verses to be remembered more than 65 years later. Whenever an appropriate refrain comes to mind up go her arms and she starts her recitation. I am afraid we tend to laugh and say 'Here she goes again,' but our admiration is none the less for an astounding memory and a deep love of the beauty of nature.

One year our father thought it would be a treat for us to visit other popular seaside resorts, so we had outings to Margate, Ramsgate and Clacton. We anticipated these outings with excitement and we enjoyed the hustle and bustle, the shops and amusements, but my sister voiced all our thoughts as we stood on one over-crowded beach. She rubbed her tired face with little brown hands and tearfully wailed 'I don't like it. It's not my Nanny's sea!'

Celebration

Came the year of the Golden Wedding. This was in June and the whole family assembled. I cannot remember any details of the preparations, but obviously all the mums had been very busy, each one providing some part of the feast. The weather was beautiful and no doubt we all wished we could stay for longer than the weekend. Trestle tables and forms were borrowed and set up in the front room, which necessitated removing the door to the hallway. I don't know why or if it gave more space, but the uncles obviously felt it was an occasion for causing as much disturbance as possible. So with the ladies endeavouring to lay-up tables, the men must take off the door!

I did not count the number who sat down to tea that afternoon. No doubt someone had, but we were all there, including the Norwich relations. Just one cousin was away on National Service, and we all drank his health.

There was a table full of presents and cards from family and neighbours, but I can only recall one gift, a dressing table set, crocheted in deep-gold silk, which today still graces my bedroom, having been passed on to my husband and me.

I have a few vivid memories of that weekend, but no details or continuity. Like a series of photographs, certain events stand out against a blurred background.

The war had not been over for more than three or four years and it was probably quite an effort to acquire ham, dried fruit and icing sugar ; even butter was still on ration; but the tables were well laden and colourful with fresh green salads.

My first picture is of Nan showing off her brand new shining gold wedding ring. 'He's made an honest woman of me at last,' she chuckled as grandad stood quietly by, for once not saying a great deal.

Amidst all the chat and comings and goings it was not noticed that grandad had slipped away. 'Where's father?' someone said. 'Over the garden feeding his rabbits, I expect,' they surmised. A little later in the morning, the latch on the back gate clicked and in came grandad almost hidden behind the most enormous bunch of flowers which he shyly presented to his wife. She received it with a gentle laugh. 'Married 50 years and he brings me stinging nettles!' Sure enough as we crowded round, we saw that the bouquet was made up entirely of wild flowers, including flowering nettles. He had been out in the hedgerows and had picked every kind of flower he could find. It was an absolute picture of pink, red, white and cream blossoms, still damp with the morning dew and framed with a few fronds of fresh-smelling ferns. No exotic blooms could match the simple beauty of that armful of English country flowers, or have conveyed any deeper message than their simplicity. Nan understood and her tender smile belied her words as she looked at grandad, his eyes moist and his moustache quivering, with the emotion he fought to hide. 'Silly old fool!' she murmured.

So the day went on with banter and laughter, eating and drinking. The happy couple were photographed in the back garden under a bower of cream roses, Nan clasping her bouquet of 'nettles'. Unfortunately it was not a good snap, but it is the only tangible memory we possess.

After the wedding breakfast, grandad went through his repertoire of songs. Standing amongst the family crowded into the little front room he sang 'Thora', one of his favourites, then the long saga of 'The Farmer's Boy.' He still remembered the many verses of the moving tale, his now somewhat tremulous voice giving full feeling to the simple yet heart-rending words. We all joined in the choruses, laughing to cover the lumps in our throats. Then, clasping his fists tightly to his sides and fixing his eyes straight ahead, he sang 'My Old Dutch', supplanting 50 years for the written 40.

There was no possible way we could all sleep at Number 9 that night, so bedrooms had been borrowed from friendly neighbours. One along the passageway, two or three at Miss Leggatt's opposite, and my cousin and I shared a room across the way in the road which ran at right angles to our grandparents.' From this back bedroom we could see the front of Number 9. Our parents and another aunt and uncle were allocated Miss Leggatt's rooms.

These were in a tall, gaunt house, with three storeys, a novelty in itself, especially as I recall you had to pass through an upstairs sitting room to reach the staircase leading to the third floor. This room had three or four doors, all varnished and grained, with large white porcelain door-knobs, which I found most confusing and I invariably walked into a cupboard. It was, like its owner, extremely old fashioned, but filled with interesting and good quality pieces of furniture, glass and china. Miss Leggatt had about her the same air of old fashioned elegance; she was always well dressed, perfumed and had her face 'made up'; which alone made her stand apart from her neighbours. She was a very kind person and allowed me to keep up my piano practice on her dreadfully old and worn instrument. It was completely out of tune, and still boasted brass candlesticks on its fret-work facia, backed with faded silk. I was very happy to slip over occasionally and play on its yellowed ivory keys, in the quiet, sun-filled room which smelled of polish, varnish and the faint mustiness of old furniture. This was combined with the gas, which was the only means of lighting they possessed.

I believe the younger children, my sister among them, were put to sleep at Nan's, and as the evening wore on we all began to drift towards our various beds, leaving our parents to finish tidying up and have a last cup of tea.

I went over the road with my eldest cousin and we climbed into bed, quietly discussing the excitement of the day. I missed being able to watch the sweep of the beam from the lighthouse, for this room faced the opposite direction, and thought of my sister in our usual bedroom. It was funny being so near but in different houses.

Just as we were beginning to drift into the silence before sleep comes, we were roused by the very faint sounds of 'music'. Clambering out of bed we slipped to the window and kneeling on the floor we peered over the gardens and across the road, just as a small procession appeared from our grandparents' passageway. It was a perfect picture in the moonlight. Six of our mothers and fathers, in single file, each with a lighted candle, were solemnly crossing the road and quietly singing 'Jesus Bids us Shine', accompanied, of course, by the occasional giggle, and 'Shush' from the others. It finished the day perfectly for the two watchers at the window.

The following morning everything was cleared away, the door put back, the house straightened and the remaining food divided. There was a lot of good-natured rivalry over a half of cucumber and who should claim it. Eventually Auntie Gertie won the day and bore it home in triumph. For years after she laughed about that cucumber. So much fuss was made over it and it turned out to be so bitter no one could eat it, and she had to throw it away. It had been carefully carried for more than 100 miles!!

Looking Back

 Family gatherings of this sort, of course, encouraged the 'Do you remember?' stories. As children we did not pay too much attention to the conversations going on around us. We had much more interesting things to do than listen to the reminiscing of our elders, but over the years we picked up enough to wonder at the full stories behind the comic and sometimes tragic tales.

My mother speaks of the day war was declared, the 1914-18 one, when a regiment of young soldiers were encamped on a field not far from their house, and as news of the outbreak of hostilities reached them, a great cheer resounded down the hill and a shower of berets, their white cockades flashing in the sun, were hurled into the air. My mother was only seven years old but the image remains in her mind, the bronzed young men in a field of poppies, cheering to know they were going to have the chance to fight for their country. Full of patriotic fervour the children would line the streets to see them march away, cheering and waving their little flags. Looking back, after living through two world wars, she might well sigh at the innocence and naivety of those days.

Grandmother, like many another, left to care for her children whilst her husband fought in the trenches, opened up her front room to the young soldiers, making them hot soup and bread, giving then a bed, before they too were shipped overseas. The children, of course, were delighted with all the extra fun and attention they came in for, the men no doubt missing their own families.

By the time war ended grandad had been discharged from the army, reasonably well after six months in a convalescent home, although bronchitis plagued him for the rest of his life. About this time grandmother was taken seriously ill and admitted to the small cottage hospital. The nature of her illness was never discussed in front of her children and we can only assume she had suffered a miscarriage, far too delicate a subject for open discussion.

Her condition must have given rise to anxiety for her recovery and her children were allowed to visit her, the first children ever permitted to do this, a somewhat dubious honour. However, this did prove to be her turning point for the better. 'I had to get well again,' she said in later years 'for the sake of those little faces looking at me.' Soon after her return home a family portrait photograph was taken, a copy of which we now possess; grandad looking very smart and well groomed, surrounded by his growing family, grandmother, a little pale, but well on the road to recovery.

There were all sorts of memories connected with the family weddings; how they all squeezed into the little house and the fun over the crowded sleeping arrangements. There were beds in every room. Nan swears she spent one such night sitting on a slop pail, because there was just no room anywhere else, although we felt this must be an exaggeration.

My mother and her brother had a double wedding. A Sunday was chosen, as most of the men-folk had to work Saturday mornings and then travel to Cromer. All went well, everyone gathering at the church early Sunday morning, everyone except the vicar. He had overlooked the occasion and the brides had to drive around the block whilst he was roused from his bed and hurried to the church.

After the wedding breakfast all the young people gathered on the beach for a game of cricket before the party broke up, the couples going directly to their new homes and work as usual on Monday. Large receptions and honeymoons were impossible, but what a happy, simple day to start a good life together.

Easter Adventure

Two or three years after the war ended, when I was around twelve or thirteen, our father decided to trust himself on a bicycle once again. My sister and I had acquired second-hand bikes which dad had made roadworthy for us. He was always checking over brake blocks, cables, chains, tyres and so on. We used them to visit our friends, pop to the shops and library, and were now wishing to go further afield. He thought it would be fun to venture forth all together, so one weekend he went out and bought two brand new machines, one for mum and one for himself.

We were green with envy. They were only the normal all-black roadsters - no racing machines for them - but the paint was gleaming, the spokes and handlebars shining, saddle and bags giving off the warm scent of newly-polished leather. The greatest joy was the Sturmey-Archer three-speed set in the back wheel of each, with a little lever on the frame, to change gear. It made such a difference. Our old things just plodded along at the set gear ratio and your legs really had to do all the work. To get on to a long flat stretch of road on one of the new bikes, and be able to slip into top gear, was marvellous. Just a slow steady rhythm of the legs kept the pedals turning and the wheels seemed to fly across the surface of the road, making the tyres sing along with the heavy tick, tick, tick from the back wheel. This for the moment was our mother's pleasure. Our young legs worked hard on the old bikes until the day came, a couple of years later, when we too were treated. Then we became the envy of our friends, with our stylish green and chrome semi-racing machines. They had narrow saddles and three-speeds, controlled by a flick of a lever on the dropped handlebars. But these were in the future and for now we were content to prepare sandwiches, pack them in our baskets on the front and set off with mum and dad on fine weekends into the Essex countryside.

Once clear of Hornchurch and Romford we had the choice of many miles of highway and byway, reasonably free from traffic.

We covered a good few miles in the course of a day out, never rushing, just enjoying the exercise and fresh air. My sister cheated quite shamelessly; whilst we three bent over our handlebars, leg muscles flexing and straining, she would prop her feet on the front of the frame, guide herself with one hand and with the other hang onto the tail of dad's coat. Sitting bolt upright, as he puffed and pulled her along, she would gaze over the hedges, chatting about the animals in the fields and smiling at anyone we passed. In turn she made them smile as she sailed along, quite unconcerned.

We visited Epping Forest, Theydon Bois, Southend, Warley, Brentwood, Ingatestone and all the surrounding area, enjoying our lunch in a meadow, sitting in the shade, perhaps perched on an old tree trunk, playing amongst the buttercups and daisies. We would come home tired and sticky, dad and I with red noses and me with sun-burned knees and arms, if I was not careful. We became very proud of ourselves and the number of miles we could cover in a day without pushing ourselves too hard.

'I reckon I could cycle to Cromer,' I boasted one evening at dinner.

'Oh, you think so, do you?' said my father

'I bet you wouldn't dare!' I countered.

'Right, my girl! I'll take you up on that,' was dad's reply.

My mother was concerned, but after planning sensibly it was decided we would make our grand trip the coming Easter. My mother and sister did not consider themselves adequate cyclists and went to an aunt's for the weekend, where we could contact them by telephone.

We left Hornchurch about eight on the Thursday evening before Good Friday. Dad had taught me to read a map and we had marked out our route. I wore my school tennis dress with a jumper, plus a raincoat for the night ride.

Getting up Brook Street hill at Brentwood was our first struggle and in keeping to the kerb, I put my front wheel down a very deep drain, almost throwing myself off as well as giving the wheel a severe jarring. My father was not pleased and told me, quite severely, to keep out of the gutters. However, we soon forgot this incident and pedalled happily side by side through the evening air.

The A12 at this time was little more than country lanes joining up the villages, with not a dual carriageway in sight. After Brook Street there were only about two other nasty hills between us and the coast, although landscapes that appear to be quite flat can still have a few nasty drags when on the saddle of a bike. I was riding my mother's cycle on this occasion and revelling in having the three-speed. Into top gear and we fairly flew through the now silent villages, our headlamps faintly picking out the road ahead of us.

At Washbrook we paused for a hot drink from our flask, resting on the little green in front of the post office. As we stood sipping our tea the curtain at an upstairs window twitched.

'Someone's watching us!' I whispered.

'I expect they're wondering what a girl and man are up to in the middle of the night,' said my father. I giggled. 'Wouldn't they be disappointed to know you're my father. They probably think we're a couple eloping!'

On our bikes again and round the next corner to meet the most awful hill, the road twisting and curving as it climbed to the top; as we set off a large lorry appeared from the opposite direction, making its way down, its headlamps blazing in our eyes and we cowering into the hedge as its brakes shrieked in their attempt to hold back the load. It was soon past and we continued on our way in the stunning silence which followed it. The night was very dark now, turning colder, but fortunately dry.

As the hours passed the moon rose, lighting our way. We stopped again for a rest and a Mars bar. Sitting on a five-barred-gate, looking at the bright, moon-lit sky, silvering the earth below, I wanted to sing 'Ain't much sense, Sitting on a fence, All by yourself in the moonlight,' and the tune ran with me as we pushed on into the Suffolk countryside. We did not speak a great deal; we were quite companionable without a lot of chatter.

Now I was beginning to feel a bit chilly, even with the heat generated by exercise. I tried to keep one hand on my knee to hold the raincoat across my legs. It was a long night and the miles seemed to be passing more slowly. I learned the truth of two sayings that night. The first was 'The darkest hour is just before dawn.' With the moon high in the sky it was almost as bright as day and I kept imagining the horizon was getting brighter and the sun coming up, but the moon began to go down and the sky became dark grey and heavy. Would the sun never rise? I was so cold and hungry. We had eaten all our chocolate and the Mars bar had left me feeling sick. When and where were we going to get some breakfast?

Suddenly we realised that at last the sky was brighter and the sun was creeping up, almost without us noticing. My father was sure that on a route where so many lorries travelled there must be places for the drivers to eat, and we knew from the number passing us in the course of the night that they would be needing breakfasts. We met a farm labourer wandering to work about half past six and he informed us that there was a cafe which opened at about seven-thirty or eight o'clock, six miles up the road. Then I learned 'The longest mile is the last mile home.' What a distance was those six miles. We were so tired and saddle-sore we decided we were better off walking for a while, and this also warmed us up a little.

The Limes at Long Stratton, although a transport cafe used by the long-distance lorry drivers, was an old country house. There was a grandfather clock in the hall and polished tables and vases of flowers in the large, cool dining room. We were greeted warmly when we rang the bell at a quarter to eight. 'Come on in, we don't serve breakfast till eight, but by the time you've had a wash and tidy-up, it'll be on the table. Bacon and eggs, toast and marmalade all right?' All right? It sounded like food for the gods, and it was. It was cooked to perfection, with masses of fresh toast and thick, tangy marmalade. We sat at a table for two in the morning sun, fresh table cloth and a pot of tea to make dad's eyes twinkle.

The miserable pair who had walked the last six miles were left well behind. The lady of the house showed great interest in our little adventure, and having cleared all that she had set before us we again mounted our steeds, excitement once more driving us towards our goal. We were now only twelve miles outside Norwich and once through the city we felt we were really on the home stretch. Twenty-two miles through the beautiful Norfolk spring-time, with the sun now high and warm. Easter must have been late that year as it turned out to be quite a heat-wave. Again the last few miles seemed to take much longer, two or three miles dragging uphill before we turned the last corner to see the familiar road ahead. This was the first time we had experienced the journey by road. Our view had always been from the train. Past the water tower, under the railway bridge and there was the lighthouse, gleaming white in the sunshine. Swooping past the 'Suffield', and now we could free-wheel down the hill, round the corner past 'Vincent's' and brake outside Number 9. No one knew we were coming as we were afraid they might worry about us. With wobbly legs we pushed our cycles up the passageway, grinning at each other as we yelled 'Pour it out!"

Good gracious me! Where have you two come from?' Nan scuttled out of the scullery, wiping her hands on her pinny. 'Where's Peggy and little Janet?' She peered over our shoulders to see if the others were coming up the passage. Breathlessly we explained we were on our own, and had cycled through the night. She took a little convincing, then said 'I knew something was going to happen this weekend. My grandson came and took me to the pictures last night and I said then that that was so unusual, something was bound to be going to happen!' My father laughed and said he always knew she was an old witch.

Into the house we staggered. A cup of tea and very soon a meal appeared from somewhere. I sat on the old couch and knew nothing until I awoke to see one of my young cousins laughing at me. I had literally fallen asleep sitting upright.

We had a lazy weekend, after telephoning to say we had arrived safely, and set off again about four on the Sunday afternoon. My father had arranged for us to stay at The Limes and complete our journey on the Monday. We had supper in the quiet dining room, for as it was the holiday weekend we were the only guests. After reading one or two boring magazines we went up for an early night. I had been given a dear little room with a single bed, a new experience as I had always shared a double bed with my sister. Father had a whole dormitory to himself, rows of little beds down one side of a long, narrow room. I don't know which one he chose!

We breakfasted early and then strolled out into the gardens before repacking our cycle bags and setting off on the 90 miles between us and home. The gentleman who owned the house called us over to see his primroses. He was experimenting on variations in colour, size and shape of petal. The whole garden was a mass of primroses of every colour imaginable. He showed us round, pointing out the various shades and the way he was producing all the different varieties. My father was fascinated and although I could not understand the technicalities I enjoyed looking at all the clusters of cream, yellow, pink, mauve, blue, white and red. One I have always remembered was a tiny, creamy-white bloom with a saw-toothed edge to the petal, making it appear like a cluster of tiny stars. They were being sent to nurseries in Lincolnshire, I believe, and I have often wondered if they were the first strains of the species we now call primulas.

It was a very peaceful start to an Easter Monday morning and we eventually dragged ourselves away and climbed into the saddle. Our journey home must have been quite uneventful, for nothing stands out in my mind. There was more traffic on the road and a quite a number of other cyclists. The sun was warm, our woollies of the night were packed away and our noses and arms grew redder as the day progressed. We turned the last corner during the early evening. My mother and sister must have been watching for us, as they came running down the path to the gate with great big smiles on their faces. I waved proudly, announcing the return of the conquering heroes.

The following Easter we repeated the ride, with another friend of the family, but the weather was not so kind to us. The air was cold with a twisty wind and, although we completed the journey down, when we reached Norwich on the return we decided to give up and go by train. My father had to dig deep into his pocket for the fares, which could not have made him very happy, but the weather, which had started the day very windy and grey, deteriorated even further and we arrived back at Romford after very heavy rain.

My father made the journey by cycle twice more after this. He sent us all off by train for our next summer holidays, and came by road himself. I know it meant the saving of one train fare, which was a strong consideration, but I am also sure that he really enjoyed the quiet hours of exercise through the peaceful countryside.

Continuity

As we all grew older these large family holidays began to break up. Some of the grandchildren were leaving school, making new friends and taking separate holidays from the family. We all visited our grandparents, but now with our own friends and at different times. Gradually the school friends gave way to our future partners. I think we all carry fond memories of our courting days in Cromer. Nan was considered to be a suitable chaperone by our parents and we were more than happy to introduce our boy and girl friends to her. She would never interfere or comment on our plans or activities unless consulted, and never showed any favouritism, we were all treated with the same kindness and affection. Some summers she must have thought she might as well have been running a boarding house, as we all tried to book our week or fortnight with her. Grandad said (with a grin) that he was glad when winter came and he could have the house to himself again.

My husband and I bought our engagement ring at the local jewellers, in the High Street, during our second holiday together, and went straight home so that Nan and grandad might be the first to admire it and hear our news. They warmly wished us happiness, especially as our parents knew of our intentions and had given us their blessings.

We had an evening at the theatre together during our last few days holiday, but on the morning we were due to leave my grandmother did not feel well and returned to bed. The doctor was sent for and we realised this was not just a matter of being under the weather. He astounded us by saying she had suffered a very serious heart attack and 'if' she came through the next 24 hours would most likely be an invalid for the rest of her life. Grandad was devastated. I did not want to leave him, but as auntie and uncle had cycled over and decided to stay with him, it was best we went home to enable my mother to come and help also.

It was a very sad journey, knowing the news we carried, and how we were going to change the 'welcome home' smiles to anxious sadness.

We had not been in long, our news broken, our own holiday pushed into the background, as we made quiet plans for our mother to go off as soon as possible, when my future father-in-law called in to say he had received a telephone message from my uncle and would my father ring back as soon as possible. Dad went straight off with him, and we all sat numb, waiting for his return. He had no need to speak when he came in. We read it in his face and our tears flowed uncontrollably. Our dear grandmother had died.

Our mother went off the next morning to be with her father and family. We had all been knocked sideways with the suddeness of our loss. There had been no warning of ill health, and although common sense told us our grandparents were not getting any younger, they had not shown any signs of getting older. This was the first close member of the family we had experienced losing and it left a mark on our lives. Would going to Cromer be the same now?

After the funeral our mother returned, quiet and sad. The shock took its toll but, as she said, it was far better than seeing her mother a helpless invalid. It had not been in her nature to be inactive and have to rely on others to care for her.

Grandad was being cared for by the auntie and uncle who lived nearby and eventually they moved in and shared his home with him.

I was surprised when, on her return, my mother handed me a parcel of little trinkets, belated engagement presents from the family. They did not wish our happiness to be forgotten; and also with them a special parcel from grandad containing the gold silk dressing table set, the set of fish knives and forks which I had been bidden to clean for my gradmother, and, carefully wrapped against breakage, the 'Boy and Girl' ornaments I had loved so much as a child. 'Your Granny always said they were to be yours,' and he had wasted no time in carrying out her wishes. I was deeply touched that he had been able to remember me in his time of sorrow.

Things did change, of course. The house was not quite the same, but auntie made us welcome, and we had one or two more holidays there, and we still loved Cromer and the surrounding districts. We were, however, all growing up now, getting married and setting up our own homes. Grandfather was present at all our weddings, still a lively, happy little man, proud to be guest of honour and share his grandchildren's happiness, and later to meet his new great-grandchildren. He was, as always, immaculate in his dress, his hair 'quiffed', moustache twirled and fresh flower in his buttonhole. When we commented on his smartness he would quip 'Anything suits good-looking people!'

Sadly as he reached his eighties circulation trouble caused him to lose both his legs and his remaining years had to be spent in a wheelchair. What frustration this must have brought to such an active person, but he did all he possibly could to care for himself, pushing himself from room to room. Auntie and uncle were magnificent in their care of him, and whenever we saw him he was bright and cheerful, but it could not always have been easy for any of them, and only they know how often tempers must have become frayed and tensions had to be smoothed over. He enjoyed being pushed out in the warm weather, even left to sit in the sun and pass the time of day with old cronies or chat to anyone who cared to pause a while. He was never at a loss for conversation, and everyone knew Mr. Muirhead.

Now our holiday plans were taking us further afield and our trips to Cromer were more often by car for the day to give grandfather a run round his old haunts and call somewhere for his favourite 'pint'. This caused much hilarity one Christmas time when we had spent some time at one of his favourite local bars. Everyone was so pleased to see 'old Jumbo' out with his family and he was in high spirits, particularly as he had been indulging in the special Christmas brew, and of course the time came when he required a toilet. It was impossible for him to reach the one on the premises in a wheelchair, but the King's Head, opposite was quite convenient. So to grandfather's delight he was wheeled from one bar to the other just to use the toilet, and then back to continue his party. Such was his popularity and charm no adverse comments were made and everyone enjoyed the joke.

It was decided, on one of these day trips, that it would be a nice break for everyone to take him back with us to stay with our parents for a few weeks. We piled the boot of the car up with wheelchair, commode and other necessary items for his comfort and popped him in the back seat with my mother and sister. Fortunately the car on that occasion had a three-seater front seat and column gear-change, so I was able to squeeze in with my father and husband, who was driving. Grandad was delighted with this sudden holiday and kept us regaled with his stories and jokes on the way home. We stopped for fish and chips, which he happily ate, vowing them the best he'd tasted for years, and then he sang all the old songs, with us joining in, for the rest of the journey.

It was pleasant having him around for those weeks, although sad to see him so dependent; but he was still the life and soul of the party.

Soon after this auntie and uncle acquired a bungalow which made life much more simple for them all. My sister and I were both expecting our first babies by now and before we could make another visit, we heard grandfather had died, and an era had passed.

Now, however, we had our own little ones to think about and when it came to planning holidays, what better than to take them back to the places we knew and loved so well.

No grandparents now to give us open house for a month. One or two weeks at a guest house were the best we could manage. Then chalets were built, not so very far from our grandparents old home. Each year we would take one or sometimes two of these 'little wooden houses' as our children called them. They came to look upon them as their 'home' in Cromer, as we had Number 9. They too ran and played with their cousins and a dog. A smaller party, but we had fun, playing cricket, flying aeroplanes and kites, challenging each other to games on the putting greens.

If we suggested another holiday resort for a change we were cried down. 'But we always go to Cromer!' Why should we argue; we were happy and knew they were too.

Gradually over the years as they too have now grown up, we have had other holidays, but always there has been the anxious question 'But, we are going to Cromer as well, aren't we?'

Many things have changed, some not for the better, but the sea, beach, cliffs, hills and woods are much the same. They all hold so many fond memories, over so many years. My mother growing up with her brothers and sisters, courting, marrying, going back with us, her children to enjoy the same pleasures, and we in our turn to introduce our own family, who have also grown to love the countryside, and now they too have their own stories and memories to laugh over.

All our recollections are different but we all share the same happy affection. Bridging the years, and taking pride of place on our mantle-shelf, we have those delicate china ornaments, given, and cared for, with love. Presents from my Norfolk grandmother, memories of those seaside days.